Understanding Ideas
Advanced reading skills

Michael Swan

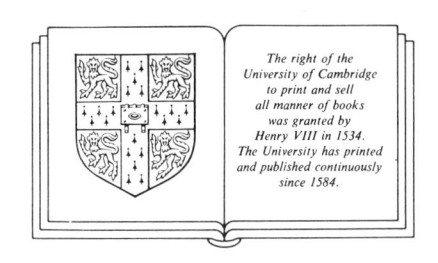

Cambridge University Press
Cambridge
New York   Port Chester
Melbourne   Sydney

Published by the Press Syndicate of the University of Cambridge
The Pitt Building, Trumpington Street, Cambridge CB2 1RP
40 West 20th Street, New York, NY 10011, USA
10 Stamford Road, Oakleigh, Melbourne 3166, Australia

© Cambridge University Press 1976

First published 1976
Fourteenth printing 1990

Printed in Great Britain by the
University Press, Cambridge

ISBN 0 521 21146 8 Student's Book
ISBN 0 521 22133 1 Teacher's Book
ISBN 0 521 22066 1 Cassette

Copyright

The law allows a reader to make a single copy of part of a book for purposes of private study. It does not allow the copying of entire books or the making of multiple copies of extracts. Written permission for any such copying must always be obtained from the publisher in advance.

Contents

Preface v

Acknowledgements vi

Notes for teachers 1

Section A: Basic reading technique

Teaching unit 1: How to read a text 5
Night sister 5

Practice unit 1.1: Cleaner 7

Practice unit 1.2: Race riot 9

Practice unit 1.3: Chimpanzees 13

Practice unit 1.4: Physical fitness 16

Teaching unit 2: Guessing unknown words 18
Baggy pants 19

Practice unit 2.1: Driver escapes through car boot 20
Pidgin English 21

Practice unit 2.2: Blue film 24

Practice unit 2.3: The front tail 28
Waiting for the lorry 29

Section B: Open-ended tests and summary-writing

Teaching unit 3: Open-ended tests 33
Trafalgar Square Rally 34

Practice unit 3.1: The reconciliation 36

Practice unit 3.2: The pistol 38

Practice unit 3.3: Snowball and Napoleon 40

Teaching unit 4: Introduction to summary 42
Just leave the keys in, sir 43
Encounter groups 43
Fictions 44

Practice unit 4.1: School and life 45

Practice unit 4.2: The eternal flaming racket of the female 46

Practice unit 4.3: Helping black teenagers to read 48

Teaching unit 5: Writing summaries 51
War 51

Practice unit 5.1: Summerhill education and standard education 53

Contents

Practice unit 5.2: Hypnosis 56

Practice unit 5.3: The Alcatraz manifesto 57

Practice unit 5.4: The marriages that Britain splits up 60

Practice unit 5.5: Nightmare in a California jail 62

Section C: Practice tests

Practice test 1: Factory life – a student's experience 65

Practice test 2: Who's crazy? 68

Practice test 3: Control units 72

Practice test 4: American finds real world in Africa 76

Practice test 5: Women's prison goes pop 79
What do prisons do? 81

Practice test 6: The politics of housework 83

Practice test 7: Violence 85

Practice test 8: How the West was lost 87

Practice test 9: Goodbye to the cane 89

Practice test 10: Schoolbooks and the female stereotype 90

Section D: Special forms of English

1 Telegrams 93
2 Instructions 94
3 Newspaper headlines 94

Preface

This is a new kind of comprehension course. Its purpose is not simply to provide practice material, but to *teach*, progressively and systematically, the various skills which are necessary for successful reading comprehension. The book contains:

Five teaching units. These provide lesson material (explanations and exercises) on various aspects of comprehension work, such as basic reading technique, guessing unknown words and writing summaries.

Eighteen practice units. These contain texts and comprehension questions (both multiple choice and open-ended) designed to give practice on the points dealt with in the teaching units.

Ten practice tests. These provide additional material which can be used for testing, assessing progress, or general revision.

A section on special forms of English. This gives training in understanding the special syntax of telegrams, instructions and newspaper headlines.

The course is designed for advanced (or 'post-intermediate') students of English as a foreign language. The book assumes a starting level just after the Cambridge First Certificate in English. It can be used for the first half of a Proficiency examination course, but it is equally suitable for comprehension work with non-examination candidates.

The texts cover a wide range of different types of modern English writing, and have been specially selected for the interest and variety of their subject matter and style. Most of them can be used not only for comprehension work, but also as a basis for other language-teaching activities such as class discussion or intensive vocabulary work.

A detailed description of the purpose and structure of the book, together with suggestions for its use, is given in 'Notes for teachers'.

M.S.

Acknowledgements

The author and publisher are grateful to the following for permission to reproduce quoted passages:

p. 9, Reprinted by permission of Penguin Books Ltd © Gus John, Derek Humphrey 1971; p. 13, Thames & Hudson Ltd; p. 16, Reprinted by permission of Penguin Books Ltd © Queen's Printer, Canada 1958, 1960; p. 19, Mirror Group Newspapers; p. 20, Guardian Newspapers Ltd; p. 21, Mr Gary Jennings and Curtis Brown Ltd; p. 24, Mr L. Deighton; p. 28, Jonathan Cape Ltd and Glidrose Productions Ltd; p. 34, Faber & Faber Ltd and John Osborne; p. 36, Reprinted by permission of A. D. Peters & Co. Ltd; p. 38, Wm Collins Sons & Co. Ltd; p. 40, Mrs Sonia Brownell Orwell and Secker & Warburg; p. 43, Hodder & Stoughton Ltd; p. 43, Reprinted by permission of Penguin Books Ltd © Carl R. Rogers 1970; p. 44, Wm Collins Sons & Co. Ltd; p. 45, Hodder & Stoughton Ltd; p. 46, Faber & Faber Ltd and John Osborne; p. 48, Reproduced from *The Times* by permission; p. 51, Yale University Press; p. 53, From *Summerhill: A Radical Approach to Child Rearing* by A. S. Neill © 1960 Hart Publishing Co., New York; p. 56, Reprinted by permission of Penguin Books Ltd © H. J. Eysenck 1957, 1958; p. 60, Reproduced from *The Sunday Times* by permission; p. 65, *Militant*; p. 68, *The Observer*; p. 72, Guardian Newspapers Ltd; p. 79, *The Guardian* and The Press Association; p. 81, the Estate of Sinclair Lewis and Jonathan Cape Ltd; p. 85, Mr Howard Zinn; p. 87, *The Observer*; p. 89, Reproduced from *The Times Educational Supplement* by permission; p. 90, Mr Bart Barnes and the *Washington Post*; p. 94, IPC Magazines Ltd; p. 94, Smith & Nephew Ltd.

Every effort has been made to reach copyright holders; the publishers would be glad to hear from anyone whose rights they may have unwittingly infringed.

Notes for teachers

What exactly is 'reading comprehension'?

If we say that a student is 'good at comprehension', we mean that he can read accurately and efficiently, so as to get the maximum of information from a text with a minimum of misunderstanding. We may also mean (though this is not quite the same) that he is able to show his understanding by re-expressing the content of the text – for instance, by writing sentences or paragraphs in answer to questions, or by summarising the text.

Language is not the only factor in successful comprehension: some students who speak and write English very well are poor at this kind of work, and of course people may be bad at comprehension even in their own mother tongue.

Some of the reasons for failure in comprehension are connected with defective reading habits. Not all students read efficiently, even in their own language, and there are several things that can go wrong.

a) Some students find it difficult to 'see the wood for the trees'. They may read slowly and carefully, paying a lot of attention to individual points, but without succeeding in getting a clear idea of the overall meaning of a text.
b) Other students (especially those who read quickly) do not always pay enough attention to detail. They may have a good idea of the general meaning of the text, but misunderstand particular points. Sometimes, by overlooking an important small word (for instance a conjunction, a negation, a modal verb) they may get a completely false impression of the meaning of a part of the passage.
c) Some students are 'imaginative readers': especially if they know something about the subject, or have strong opinions about it, they may interpret the text in the light of their own experience and ideas, so that they find it difficult to separate what the writer says from what they feel themselves.

Other types of comprehension problem arise directly from the text.

d) Some writers favour a wordy and repetitive style; practice is needed to be able to 'see through' the words to the (often very simple) ideas which underlie them.
e) Words and expressions which the student does not know obviously present a problem (unless he is working with a dictionary). However, students do not always realise how easy it is to guess many unknown words simply by studying the context. Some students, indeed, are so disturbed by unfamiliar vocabulary that their comprehension of the whole passage suffers as a result.

Finally, some 'comprehension' examinations test skills which go beyond the limits of comprehension proper. Summary-writing is a good example of this: most students, even those with a good knowledge of the language and adequate comprehension skills, need special training in order to be able to summarise effectively.

Notes for teachers

In this book, the various problems referred to above are separated out, and specific training is provided in each of the skills involved.

Structure of the book

The book contains four main sections. These are:

Section A   Basic reading technique and multiple choice tests
Section B   Open-ended tests and summary-writing
Section C   Practice tests
Section D   Special forms of English

Sections A and B each contain teaching units. A teaching unit is designed for classwork, and contains introductory explanations and exercises on a specific element of comprehension technique (e.g. accurate reading; writing summaries).

Each teaching unit is followed by a number of practice units (suitable for classwork or homework), containing texts and questions. The practice units give further work on the point dealt with in the teaching unit, together with general comprehension practice and revision of points dealt with earlier.

The practice tests in Section C are similar in design to practice units, but a little more difficult. They can be used at the end of a course for various purposes – for instance: a) to assess progress   b) to screen potential examination candidates   c) for revision work. Alternatively, they might be used during a course as supplementary practice material for students who want to do extra work.

Section D provides explanations and exercises on certain uses of English which present particular comprehension difficulties because of the special syntax involved (telegrams, instructions and newspaper headlines).

How to use the book

Obviously the exercises and materials in the book can be used in various ways, and experienced teachers will adopt whatever approach is best suited to their style of teaching and the needs of their classes. The following notes are intended merely as suggestions.

a) *Progression.* Sections A and B constitute a progressive teaching programme for comprehension skills, beginning with basic reading technique and finishing with summary-writing. It is therefore advisable, on the whole, to work through the teaching units 'from left to right' – that is, in the order in which they come in the book.

b) *Teaching units and practice units.* After doing a teaching unit, there is no need to do all the practice units which follow. One at least should be done straight away (either for homework or in the next comprehension lesson); if time allows and more practice is needed, teachers may wish to do a second practice unit before going on to the next teaching unit. Others can be dropped, or used for revision at a later stage. Practice units in each set vary a little in length and level, and there are great differences of style and subject matter, so it is worth looking at all of them to see which is most suitable for a particular class. Note that in the section on writing summaries there are more practice units than usual in order to give adequate work on this point, which many students find especially difficult.

c) *Handling a teaching unit in class.* As well as introductory exercises on the point being taught, the teaching units contain explanations addressed directly to the students. These are not, of course, intended to replace the teacher's lesson on the point; their purpose

Notes for teachers

is rather to provide students with a simple guide to which they can refer when preparing or revising the work done in class. Teachers will decide for themselves how to present and work through the teaching unit material; three possible approaches are as follows:

(i) Begin by giving your own lesson on the relevant point (modifying or supplementing the teaching apparatus in the book to suit your own approach and the needs of the students). Then work through the exercise material in the teaching unit. This can be done orally, or students can write their answers and then discuss them. Group work can be very effective with some of the exercises: students can work together to produce answers to the questions, or they can write their answers individually and then join together into groups to compare and discuss what they have written.

(ii) If there is not much time available, ask students to prepare the lesson by reading the teaching unit at home before the class. Lesson time can then be devoted to doing the exercises and discussing the problems which arise.

(iii) If time is really short, simply give a brief lesson on the point dealt with in the unit, and ask students to read the unit and do the exercises for homework.

Note that the teaching units vary in length; with some of the longer ones, it may be necessary to spend two lessons on the unit, or to begin the unit in class and ask the students to finish it for homework.

d) *Dictionaries.* On the whole, it is advisable for students to do their comprehension classwork and homework without dictionaries. It is important for them to get used to dealing confidently with unfamiliar vocabulary (see teaching unit 2, 'Guessing unknown words'), and of course examination candidates need to practise working without reference books. Where a text contains a difficult word or expression which could hinder comprehension of the whole passage, the meaning is explained in a footnote.

Beyond comprehension

Although the passages in the book are intended to function primarily as vehicles for comprehension training, many of them deserve more than this. It seems absurd to deal with Neill's views on education, for example, purely in terms of 'What does the word *it* in line 6 refer to?' or 'Summarise the passage in a paragraph of 100 words'. Once a text like this has been thoroughly understood, and the comprehension work is finished, it should be possible to move on to other activities, such as intensive vocabulary work, semi-controlled composition, and (in many cases) discussion. The following suggestions may be helpful.

Intensive vocabulary work. The best approach here is probably to select for teaching a limited number (perhaps 10 to 20) of words and expressions from the text. These should obviously be items which the students cannot yet use correctly (though they may already understand them), but they should be common and preferably useful for speech as well as writing. If the students are going to do writing or discussion work related to the text, the words and expressions ought to be chosen with this in mind. When these words and expressions have been explained and practised, give the students time to study them and then, perhaps in the next lesson, give a 'recall test' – that is to say, ask questions to which the answers are the items that were studied.

Semi-controlled composition. Vocabulary is not usually learnt very effectively unless it is actually used to express something. A good approach is to follow up intensive vocabulary

Notes for teachers

study with a composition exercise. In this, students are asked to write about a subject similar to that of the text, so that they can use the new words and expressions to convey their own ideas. (For example, after studying *School and life*, p. 45, students could write about their own education, saying how effective they feel it was as a preparation for life.) Make sure that students understand that they are expected to use words and expressions from the text, and that they realise why this is important.

Discussion. Some of the texts can be used as a basis for discussion. This is probably most effective after vocabulary study and writing work have been done, so that students are familiar with some of the words and expressions they will need.

Grouping texts. In order to facilitate discussion and composition work, two or three texts on similar subjects can be studied in combination. Texts which could be grouped in this way are:

—practice units 1.2, 4.3, 5.3 and practice test 8 (racialism)
—the three texts in teaching unit 4 (pretences)
—practice units 4.1, 4.3, 5.1 and practice tests 9 and 10 (education)
—practice unit 5.5 and practice tests 3 and 5 (prisons)
—practice unit 5.4 and practice tests 6 and 10 (position of women)
—teaching unit 5 and practice test 7 (war and violence).

Note: contracted forms

Students are sometimes told that contractions such as *don't*, *it's*, *they'll* are only used in writing down direct speech. This is not, of course, true: contractions are common in informal written English of all kinds, and they will be found in many of the texts in this book. The instructions to students in the teaching units are deliberately written in a casual, informal style, and these too contain contractions. However, students who use the book should perhaps be warned not to use contractions themselves when a more formal style is appropriate: they should realise clearly that contractions would be out of place, for instance, in a job application or a serious essay in an examination.

Section A:
Basic reading technique

Teaching unit 1: How to read a text

In this unit you are going to practise the technique of reading a text so as to understand the meaning as clearly as possible. It is generally a good idea to read a comprehension passage at least twice: once to get an overall impression of what it's about, and then a second time to concentrate on the details. Read much more slowly than you would read a novel or a newspaper article – most people read comprehension texts far too fast. Time spent reading is saved later, because you can answer the questions more quickly and accurately.

First reading

Read the following text once, not too fast, and then do exercise a.

Night Sister

Ferzana Yusaf from Kenya is twenty-five and has been a night sister at the new Charing Cross Hospital since last April. She's in charge of up to ten wards, including two cancer wards and the kidney transplant unit. 'We did a transplant last night – the call came through from Guy's Hospital earlier saying that they'd got a suitable donor, but it took hours to locate our patient because he'd gone drinking somewhere! And he was in the operating theatre from 1 o'clock till about 5. It was quite a night, last night!'

She works eight nights on, six nights off, from 9.15 p.m., to 8 a.m. 'We get an hour off for lunch about 2 a.m....' I smiled at 'lunch'. 'Well, what else would you call roast lamb and two veg? We have another half-hour break later on, though we can drink as much tea or coffee as we like – it's very welcome about midnight, when I sometimes start feeling a bit sleepy.'

She'd worked nights before, as a student nurse, and hadn't enjoyed the experience at all. 'I was in a geriatric hospital which was rather grim. And I worked so hard that by 8 o'clock I was too tired to sleep. But it was only twelve weeks a year, and somehow I got through it.'

It's perhaps surprising, then, that she chose to work nights permanently. 'I felt I needed a change for one thing. And for another, I hope eventually to be a sister tutor (training other nurses) and the experience will be useful.' This time around she's finding it much easier – a sister's work is physically less demanding than a nurse's – and she's found she can sleep eight hours during the day. 'I do find, though, that when I've finished my eight nights it takes me three or four days to get over it. But when I go back on duty after six days off I adjust straight away – I have to.'

The only problem she has are the headaches she gets from the dim, luminous lighting in the wards – and her weight: 'I put on a lot in the first few months, but now I've taken it all off so I'm trying to fatten myself up again!' She never gets frightened, though, and rarely feels lonely. 'The odd times it's happened, when we're very quiet, it's been boredom more than loneliness. But on the whole the atmosphere is so lively at night that I'm very happy.'

During the day, she's found, there's so much going on in the wards to distract patients that nursing is very largely confined to the practicalities – dishing out medicines, fetching bedpans and so on. But during the night, when there's nothing for the patients to do but think, it becomes much more personal – psychological even. 'Patients want to talk more at night, and we have more time to listen. For me, the most rewarding thing of all is to have someone confide his fears in me and be able to reassure him.'

She hasn't found that working nights has caused too great an upheaval in her domestic life. She shares a flat in a hospital house with a nurse on a different shift, so shopping for food and visits to the launderette can be worked out between them. But she doesn't like not having time to wash her long thick black hair for eight days on the trot, and she's had to learn to cram all her socialising into six days out of a fortnight. 'I can go out between 6 and 9 on the evenings I'm working, but I don't because it doesn't feel right. I can have visitors too, but my friends are very strongly discouraged from coming before 6! After all, if I'm going to do a night's work I must get a good day's sleep.'
(From an article in *Honey* Magazine)

Exercise a

Answer the following questions without looking at the text. You can answer in a word, a short phrase, or a complete sentence, just as you like. If you have a lot of difficulty with the exercise, it probably means that you read the text too fast.

1 What sort of work does Ferzana Yusaf do?
2 Does she have a responsible position in her hospital?
3 Is she happy with her job?
4 What was the job she had before?
5 Was she happy in that job?
6 Why did she choose to do night work? (Two reasons)
7 How does she adjust to the change from night to day?
8 Does she have any problems because of doing night work?
9 What does she find is the most important difference between day and night nursing?

Second reading

Now read the text again. This time, read even more slowly, and pay special attention to points that seem difficult. Don't read a sentence until you've understood the sentence before as well as you can. If there's a word you don't know, don't waste too much time worrying about what it might mean. Look at what comes before and after, make an intelligent guess at the meaning, and then go on. When you think you're ready, try the next exercise.

Practice unit 1.1

Exercise b: Same or different?

Some of the following sentences say the same thing as part of the text; others have a different meaning. Write the numbers of the sentences, and put S (=same) or D (=different) after each one. You can look at the text if you want to.
Example:

1 *Ferzana is in charge of two cancer wards. Answer: 1S*
2 *The hospital has existed since last April. Answer: 2D*

1 Ferzana recently carried out a kidney transplant.
2 She was in the operating theatre for about four hours.
3 She works eight nights every fortnight.
4 They have a break at midnight to drink as much coffee or tea as they like.
5 She works twelve weeks a year.
6 She started night work to have a change, and for the experience.
7 This job is easier than her previous nursing post.
8 When she goes off duty she adjusts straight away.
9 She's fat.
10 She usually finds it quiet and boring at night.
11 Night nursing is more personal than day nursing.
12 She goes out between 6 and 9 on the evenings she's working.

Check your answers (you may like to discuss them with other students first). If you got several wrong, it means that you didn't pay enough attention to detail: be careful to look at *all* the words, both in the text and in the questions.

Practice unit 1.1

Read the text slowly and carefully. After the first reading, do exercise a: this will help you to see whether you have got a good general idea of what the passage says. Then read the text again, paying careful attention to detail, and do exercise b.

Cleaner

'Margaret' is married with two small children and for the last seven years has been working as a night cleaner, with one of the big contractors who provide cleaners to both private and Government office buildings all over London.

She trained as a nurse, but had to give it up when her eldest child became seriously ill with asthma. 'I would have liked to go back to it, but the shifts are all wrong for me. They work from 8 or 9 at night till 8 in the morning, and that's no good because I have to be home to get the children up and off to school. They could do it themselves, I suppose. But I don't think it's fair to expect them to.'

So she works as a cleaner instead, from 9 p.m. till 6 a.m. five nights a week – Friday and Saturday nights are free – for the princely sum of just under £20, before tax and insurance.

'It's better than it was before we had the strike last year, but I still think they should pay us more.' (A certain amount of victimisation – if that's not too strong a word – followed the strike. Hence 'Margaret' prefers not to be named.) She agrees that people who work

Practice unit 1.1

'unsocial hours' should get a bit extra, though she's pretty certain that she and the other cleaners won't! 15

The hours she's chosen to work mean that she sees plenty of the children, but very little of her husband: 'He's going to work as I get home, and I only see him for a couple of hours in the evenings.' But she doesn't think that puts any strain on the relationship: 'Secret of a happy marriage, that,' she says with a grin.

The work she does – hoovering, dusting, emptying waste-paper baskets, cleaning lavatories – isn't physically very hard. But it's not exactly pleasant, either: 'I do get irritated with people who leave their offices like pigsties – tables and desk tops are the worst, covered in sticky coffee and tea stains, with crumbs of buns and biscuits all over the place – it really can be filthy. I sometimes think people imagine their offices get cleaned by magic, by the Little People! If they thought about it and realised that people like me have to do it, perhaps they'd be a bit more careful.' 20 ... 25

The fact that she's working all night doesn't worry Margaret at all. Unlike some buildings where there's very little lighting at night – and where a cleaner who had an accident could easily not be found for hours because no one else is working on her floor – the building where she works is fully lit all night, and the women work in groups of three. 'I'm doing the job because I have to. But since I've got to be here night after night I try and enjoy myself – and I usually do, because of the other girls. We all have a good laugh, so the time never drags.'

She gets home about 6.30, gets the children ready for school, then starts on her own housework. Some days she goes to bed for two or three hours; others she doesn't go to bed at all. 'I didn't today, and I won't be able to tomorrow, either, because I'm taking my son back to his special school. But I often go two or three days without any sleep. At first I found it hard, but that was because I'd never done any cleaning before. You soon get used to it, though.' 35

You also, apparently, get used to the reaction of other people when you tell them what you do for a living. 'They think just because you're a cleaner you don't know how to read and write. I must admit, when I first started I used to think "What would my Mum and Dad say if they knew I'd been cleaning?" But I don't think that way any more. It's about the only job I can do at the moment that suits me, what with the children and everything. I don't dislike the work, but I can't say I'm mad about it. If they opened a factory round here and the hours and pay were the same as I'm getting now, then I'd rather take a job there. But it would have to be as close to my house as this place is. Because here, if my son gets ill, my husband can come straight round and fetch me. 45

'I'll give myself another year or eighteen months at the cleaning. Though what I'll do then I'm not sure. The children will be that much older, so perhaps I'll go back to nursing.' 50

It's easy to understand why she wants to do that – the work's just as hard, the pay probably not quite as good. But at least people know you can read and write.
(From an article in *Honey* Magazine)

Exercise a (first reading)

Answer the following questions without looking at the text. You can answer in a word, a short phrase, or a complete sentence, just as you like.

1   What is Margaret's job?
2   Why did she stop being a nurse?
3   Why couldn't she go back to nursing?

8

Practice unit 1.2

4 Is she well paid?
5 Have her conditions improved?
6 Is Margaret her real name?
7 Who does she see more, her children or her husband?
8 Does she mind?
9 Is her work hard?
10 What are the good sides of the job?
11 What are the bad sides?
12 Why does her son go to a special school?

Exercise b (second reading): Same or different?

Write the numbers of the sentences, followed by S (if you think the sentence says the same as the text) or D (if you think it means something different). Look at the text if you want to.

1 Margaret works from 8 or 9 at night till 8 in the morning.
2 She is paid £20 a week plus tax and insurance.
3 She used to be a nurse.
4 The strike got the cleaners more money but caused some trouble for her.
5 She's sorry she doesn't see her husband more.
6 Some people leave their offices very dirty.
7 Margaret doesn't mind working all night.
8 A cleaner had an accident in the building where Margaret works.
9 The time passes quickly because Margaret works with three other cleaners.
10 People think cleaners are badly educated.
11 In a year or two Margaret is going to return to nursing.

Practice unit 1.2

Read the text slowly and carefully. After the first reading, do exercise a: this will help you to see whether you have got a good general idea of what the passage says. Then read the text again, paying careful attention to detail, and do exercises b and c.

Race riot

'Blackie bastards!' yelled Kenneth Horsfall at three young Indian men who were leaving a cafe a few minutes after midnight. 'Blackie bastards, keep quiet and go!' he repeated. Mohammed Rashid shouted at him to stop the abuse and then attacked with his fists.
   This was the beginning of the incident which triggered off the most serious racial disturbances which have occurred so far in Britain. The date was 27 July 1969.
   Horsfall, a nineteen-year-old furniture packer, ran off to get help after exchanging blows with Rashid. A gang of white men rapidly left their homes and came down the hill to meet the Indians. How many there were is uncertain because witnesses' estimates varied. There was a running battle but the Indians – who were three in number with a fourth in the background – were outnumbered and Bhupinder Singh drew a knife which he had taken from another participant, Dian Singh Ball, during a violent argument earlier in the cafe. It was the only knife among them but it had tragic consequences.

Seeing the knife flash, Horsfall ran off to fight the other two Indians. Singh ran after him and buried the knife once into Horsfall's shoulder and once into his brain. He died in hospital at 2.20 a.m. The blood-letting stopped the fighting and the police arrested the three Indians in nearby streets within a few minutes.

The events which followed that fight are of far greater significance. Kenneth Horsfall's death happened too late for it to be reported in the morning newspapers and as the following day was Sunday there were no evening newspapers. So it was left to word of mouth to spread accounts of the killing around Burley and into other parts of Leeds. Sunday was a fine, warm day, people were out in their gardens – if they had them – or sat on their doorsteps in the sunshine, all circumstances were conducive to a high circulation of gossip. The versions of how Horsfall died grew more exaggerated as they circulated – one account had it that it was a ritual killing and forty Pakistanis had danced a triumphal war dance around his dead body !

When the public houses opened at noon the stories spread like wildfire and as they closed at the end of the lunch period violence was close. But it took another session of drinking that sultry evening for enough people to acquire courage to put their talk into action. When the pubs closed at 10.30 people began to gather in Woodsley Road quite near to the scene of the stabbing twenty-three hours earlier. There was talk of 'doing the Pakis' – throughout the whole affair people referred to the killers as Pakistanis instead of Indians. Rumour circulated in the town that coachloads of people from other parts of Leeds were coming to help in a big retaliation against the Pakistanis. As the crowd began to move forward – it numbered between 800 and 1,000 strong – there were shouts of 'We want a riot' and one woman yelled: 'We are going to smash up the Pakistani houses.' Middle-aged women were prominent in the verbal viciousness.

The police tried to persuade people to go home but the mob surged on to the cafe in Hyde Park Road, from which the three Indians had emerged when they encountered Kenneth Horsfall, and smashed its windows. The fronts of several other business premises owned by Indians and Pakistanis were also damaged. Kenneth Horsfall's father jumped onto a garden wall and said: 'It is me that is suffering. It is me that has to go to the funeral. I don't want to see anything like this and my son would not have liked it either.' No notice was taken of his appeal. Another man also addressed the crowd from a wall: 'I don't like black men either but let us go home.' The crowd swept down into Burley Lodge Road and any Pakistanis still on the street fled to the top of the hill and watched at a safe distance from behind walls. The others kept to the shelter of their homes. Stones and bottles were thrown at windows of houses which the mobsters thought had black owners but many of their targets were white-owned. A white Hillman Imp saloon parked in Burley Lodge Place, which the crowd believed belonged to a Pakistani, was overturned and set alight by eight men. In fact it belonged to a white resident. As firemen put out the blaze the cries of 'Let's get the Pakistanis' increased and police formed a human barricade to head off the mob. Nazi salutes were given and cries of 'Sieg Heil' as scuffles between the police and the crowd broke out. Four policemen were hurt making twenty-three arrests.

The anger of the white community began to turn from the Pakistanis to the police when it was realised that the police were protecting the immigrants. A police sergeant was asked: 'Why don't you black your face?' Then he was called a 'Paki-lover' and told: 'Get out of the way, it's not you we're after.' Some of the worst violence occurred when rioters tried to release men arrested by the police. The conduct of the police throughout the entire disturbances was exemplary despite considerable provocation and violence used against them. A few militants persisted in shouting 'Get the wogs' and 'Pakis go home', but by 1 a.m. the area was growing quiet. Fortunately the rumoured coachloads of

Practice unit 1.2

National Front men coming to support the white cause, and carloads of Pakistanis from nearby Bradford to defend their fellow-countrymen, either did not materialise or were headed off by community leaders.
(Abridged; from *Because They're Black* by Derek Humphrey and Gus John)

Exercise a (first reading)

Answer the following questions without looking at the text. You can answer in a word, a short phrase, or a complete sentence, just as you like.

1. What is the passage about?
2. What started the fight between Kenneth Horsfall, Mohammed Rashid and their friends?
3. What were the nationalities of the people involved?
4. How did the fight end?
5. What further serious consequence did the fight have?
6. Why was it easy for rumours to spread the next day?
7. How long after the fight did the riot start?
8. What was the purpose of the rioters?
9. What was the purpose of the police?
10. Did the rioters succeed in their aim?
11. Do the writers say that the police behaved well or badly?

Exercise b (second reading): Same or different?

Write the numbers of the sentences, followed by S (if you think the sentence means the same as the text) or D (if you think it means something different). Look at the text if you want to.

1. Horsfall's murder was the most serious racial disturbance in Britain so far.
2. Singh had taken the knife away from another Indian earlier.
3. The Indians were arrested a few minutes after 2.20 a.m.
4. The following day, exaggerated stories about the killing spread round Leeds.
5. People gathered courage for the riot by drinking in the pubs.
6. Coachloads of people came from other parts of Leeds.
7. Middle-aged women used aggressive language.
8. A crime committed by Indians led to attacks on Pakistanis, Indians and white people.
9. Twenty-three people were arrested for hurting four policemen.
10. Some of the worst violence happened when rioters who tried to release men were arrested by the police.
11. Carloads of Pakistanis from Bradford didn't reach the scene of the riot.

Exercise c (second reading): Multiple choice

For each of the following questions, you are given four possible answers. Only one is right. Choose the answer you think is correct, and write the number of the question and the letter of the correct answer. (For example, if you think the first answer to question number 1 is the right one, write 1a.)

Practice unit 1.2

1 The killing was not reported in the next day's newspapers because
a) there are no newspapers on Sundays in Britain.
b) newspaper reporters don't work on Saturdays.
c) there are no evening papers on Saturdays.
d) there are no evening papers on Sundays and the news was too late for the morning ones.

2 According to the text, Burley seems to be
a) a part of Leeds.
b) near Leeds.
c) another name for Leeds.
d) another name for Bradford.

3 Kenneth Horsfall's father
a) was so upset by his son's death that he encouraged the rioters.
b) was upset by his son's death but didn't want the riot to take place.
c) told the crowd that they did not understand how much he suffered.
d) was not seriously upset by his son's death.

4 The police
a) succeeded in preventing a serious riot.
b) succeeded in preventing all the violence that was attempted.
c) were unable to prevent any of the violence that was attempted.
d) were completely unable to control the crowd.

5 A policeman was advised to black his face
a) as a sign that he was ashamed of himself.
b) because he seemed to be on the side of the coloured people.
c) so that he would be more difficult to see.
d) so that he could spy on the Pakistanis.

6 In this passage, the writer on the whole
a) blames the Indians for what happened.
b) blames the Pakistanis.
c) blames the white people.
d) simply reports the facts.

Practice unit 1.3

Read the text slowly and carefully. After the first reading, do exercise a: this will help you to see whether you have got a good general idea of what the passage says. Then read the text again, paying careful attention to detail, and do exercises b and c.

Chimpanzees

Chimps apparently live in troops of between 20 and 50 animals. Within these troops they form small groups of varying composition; the most basic group consists of females or females plus offspring. Adult females spending much time together often turn out to be mother and daughter, or sisters. Mother and offspring live together consistently, at least for the first four or five years of life, longer than in any other primate except man. During this time the young learn from their mother and from other chimps all the complicated acquired behaviours of chimpanzee adult life. Life for the young chimpanzee is relaxed and tolerant, and an infant will spend much of its time playing with other infants, with its mother and with its brothers and sisters. After this five-year initial period, contacts with the mother are still maintained, particularly by daughters. Even sons return from time to time from their wanderings to greet their mothers affectionately.

...In the forest chimps are predominantly fruit-eaters (upon occasion they are cannibalistic!), but in open woodland they may add more protein to their diet. Males sometimes kill colobus monkeys or bush-pig; often males will gang up in a group to achieve their ends. Meat is a very choice item in chimpanzee diet and is eaten slowly and deliberately with a mouthful of leaves between each bite. It is sometimes shared out with other chimps who will beg for pieces. This food-sharing is very unusual among non-human primates; mostly it is every primate for himself. When the season is right chimps in woodlands also eat termites, and they do this by 'fishing' for them. When beginning a bout of termiting, an animal will carefully select stems or pieces of grass, trim them to the appropriate length, collect enough of them, and set out on the hunt for insects. It may pass over several termite hills if they are not ready and go on until it finds a mound ripe for fishing. Using a finger, a hole is scraped and the prepared twig inserted. Withdrawn covered with termites, it is passed carefully over the lower lip until every delicious morsel is removed, and the operation repeated. Clearly, in doing so, chimps are taking natural objects, modifying them to a standard pattern and using them for an objective which involves planning and forethought. They are, in fact, making tools. This has surprised many people, for previously man was considered to be the only tool-maker. In the chimpanzee, however, the intellectual abilities necessary for purposeful tool-making are already developed at an infra-human level. Other examples of chimp tool-use in natural surroundings have also been seen. For instance, chewed leaves are used as sponges to soak up water from holes in trees. They are also used to wipe dung or mud from the body. Stones and branches are used too in agonistic displays or when an animal is excited. They may be thrown under- or over-arm, often with considerable force and accuracy. Similar behaviour has been observed in other apes. Stones are used to open nuts too.

There are some further peculiarities of ape behaviour which are quite fascinating. Jane van Lawick-Goodall once observed a chimpanzee sitting, apparently transfixed, watching a beautiful African sunset. Can chimps have aesthetic tastes? Examples of ape art in zoos would suggest that this is certainly the case. In London Zoo chimps have learnt how to paint, always with a detectable individualistic style. They can match the compositional abilities of a three-year-old human child, before the first diagrammatic representation of

Practice unit 1.3

the face. Painting is to a high degree 'autotelic', that is to say, self-rewarding. Ape painters hate being interrupted, even for food! Jane van Lawick-Goodall has also seen what she calls a 'rain-dance', an energetic and rhythmic series of movements performed by males, watched by excited females, when there is a tropical rainstorm. 45
(From *The Evolution of Man* by David Pilbeam)

Exercise a (first reading)

Answer the following questions without looking at the text. You can answer in a word, a short phrase, or a complete sentence, just as you like.

1. As chimpanzees are described in the passage, they seem to be similar to men in three important ways. What are they?
2. What sort of groups do chimps live in?
3. How long does a baby chimp stay with its mother, and what does it do during this period?
4. Is it male or female chimps that keep the closest relationship with their mothers after growing up?
5. What do chimps eat?
6. What ways of using tools are described in the passage?
7. What forms of artistic appreciation and activity have been observed in chimps, according to the passage?

Exercise b (second reading): Same or different?

Write the numbers of the sentences, followed by S (if you think the sentence means the same as the text) or D (if you think it means something different). Look at the text if you want to.

1. The simplest social group of chimpanzees consists of mother, father and children.
2. Members of chimp families seem to be rather affectionate to each other.
3. A baby chimp spends most of its time learning and playing.
4. The kind of food chimps eat depends partly on their environment.
5. Meat is very rare in a chimpanzee diet.
6. Food-sharing is unusual among chimpanzees.
7. Sometimes they eat fish.
8. Chimpanzees have been observed to paint diagrammatic representations of the human face.

Exercise c (second reading): Multiple choice

For each of the following questions, you are given four possible answers. Only one is right. Choose the answer you think is correct, and write the number of the question and the letter of the correct answer. (For example, if you think the first answer to question number 1 is the right one, write 1a.)

1. The word 'it', in line 16, refers to
a) each bite.
b) a mouthful of leaves.

14

Practice unit 1.3

c) meat.
d) chimpanzee diet.

2 The word 'it', in line 18, refers to
a) this food-sharing.
b) the custom among non-human primates.
c) every primate.
d) diet.

3 In order to catch termites, a chimp
a) cleans the grass off a termite hill.
b) fishes them out with a 'twig' made of stems or bits of grass.
c) gets them out with its fingers.
d) uses its lower lip.

4 What is meant by 'in doing so' in line 25?
a) in repeating the operation
b) in passing the twig over the lower lip
c) in removing every delicious morsel
d) in catching termites in this way

5 'This', in line 27, refers to
a) the fact that chimps can make tools.
b) the way chimps catch termites.
c) the fact that chimps take natural objects.
d) the fact that man was previously considered to be the only tool-maker.

6 What does the writer regard as evidence of artistic capabilities in chimpanzees?
a) apparent enjoyment of a sunset
b) ability to paint
c) the 'rain-dance'
d) all three

7 In general, the passage is about
a) ways in which chimps are different from other sorts of ape.
b) ways in which chimps are different from men.
c) ways in which chimps are similar to men.
d) the way in which chimps are brought up.

Practice unit 1.4

Read the text slowly and carefully. After the first reading, do exercise a: this will help you to see whether you have got a good general idea of what the passage says. Then read the text again, paying careful attention to detail, and do exercise b.

Physical fitness

The human body is made up mainly of bone, muscle, and fat. Some 639 different muscles account for about 45 per cent of the body weight. Each of these muscles has four distinct and measurable qualities which are of interest to us:
(1) it can produce force which can be measured as strength of muscle;
(2) it can store energy which permits it to work for extended periods of time independent of circulation – this is generally referred to as *muscular endurance*;
(3) it can shorten at varying rates. This is called *speed of contraction*;
(4) it can be stretched and will recoil. This is called the *elasticity of muscle*.
The combination of these four qualities of muscle is referred to as *muscular power*.

If muscles are to function efficiently, they must be continually supplied with energy fuel. This is accomplished by the blood which carries the energy fuel from lungs and digestive system to the muscles. The blood is forced through the blood vessels by the heart. The combined capacity to supply energy fuels to the working muscles is called *organic power*.

The capacity and efficiency with which your body can function depends on the degree of development of both your muscular and organic power through regular exercise. However, the level to which you can develop these powers is influenced by such factors as the type of body you have, the food you eat, presence or absence of disease, rest and sleep. You are physically fit only when you have adequately developed your muscular and organic power to perform with the highest possible efficiency.

Heredity and health determine the top limits to which your physical capacity can be developed. This is known as your 'potential physical capacity'. This potential capacity varies from individual to individual. Most of us, for example, could train for a lifetime and never come close to running a four-minute mile simply because we weren't 'built' for it. The top level at which you can perform physically right now is called your 'acquired capacity' because it has been acquired or developed through physical activity in your daily routines.

Your body, like a car, functions most efficiently well below its acquired capacity. A car, for example, driven at its top speed of, say, 110 miles per hour uses more petrol per mile than when it is driven around 50–60 miles per hour, which is well below its capacity. Your body functions in the same way, in that the ratio of work performed to energy expended is better when it functions well below acquired capacity.

You can avoid wastage of energy by acquiring a level of physical capacity well above the level required to perform your normal daily tasks. This can be accomplished by supplementing your daily physical activity with a balanced exercise programme performed regularly. Your capacity increases as you progressively increase the load on your muscular and organic systems. Exercise will increase physical endurance and stamina thus providing a greater reserve of energy for leisure-time activities.
(From the Royal Canadian Air Force *Physical Fitness*)

Practice unit 1.4

Exercise a (first reading)

Answer the following questions without looking at the text. You can answer in a word, a short phrase, or a complete sentence, just as you like.

1 According to the passage, the human body is made up of three main components. What are they?
2 How much of the body weight is made up of muscles – half, more than half, or less than half?
3 The writer says that muscles have four different qualities. How many of them can you remember (you don't need to remember the exact words of the text)?
4 What name does the writer give to the combination of these four qualities?
5 What does blood do for the muscles?
6 According to the text, the level to which you can develop your muscular and organic powers depends on several things. Which of the following: what sort of body you have; what you eat; how old you are; whether you are well or ill; your work; rest and sleep; the condition of your heart?
7 Can you explain simply what the author means by 'potential physical capacity' and 'acquired capacity'?
8 In what way, according to the text, is the human body like a car?
9 Why does exercise make it possible to enjoy your leisure more?

Exercise b (second reading): Same or different?

Write the numbers of the sentences, followed by S (if you think the sentence means the same as the text) or D (if you think it means something different). Look at the text if you want to.

1 The human body is made entirely of bone, muscle and fat.
2 The body contains some 639 different muscles.
3 Some of these muscles are strong, some have endurance, some can work fast, and some are elastic.
4 Different muscles can shorten by different amounts.
5 All muscles can stretch.
6 The blood carries energy from the lungs to the digestive system and from there to the muscles.
7 Organic power is the ability of the heart, lungs and digestive system, all together, to supply energy to the muscles through the blood.
8 Exercise can develop both organic and muscular power.
9 Not everybody can get up to the same level of physical performance.
10 Most of us couldn't run a mile in four minutes because we're not fit enough.
11 A car uses more energy, proportionately, when it goes at 50–60 miles per hour than when it goes at top speed.
12 You should develop more fitness than you need just for your work.

Teaching unit 2: Guessing unknown words

In any comprehension text you will find words that you don't know. You can look them up in a dictionary, of course, but it's a good idea to get into the habit of doing without a dictionary as much as possible, particularly if you are preparing for an examination. In fact, if you read the text carefully and think, it's usually possible to guess the meaning of most of the words that you don't know. Look at the *context* of each word – the sentence that it's in, and the sentences that come before and after. Look to see if the word is repeated later in the text; the more often it's used, the easier it is to understand.

Unless your English is very good, you probably don't know the words 'fret' or 'bawl'. As long as they are alone, there's no way of guessing what they mean, but see what happens when they are put into a context:

1 The strings of the guitar should be pressed down just *behind*, not *on* the fret. By doing this, the string is brought firmly into contact with the metal of the fret. Notice that each time you move your finger up a fret, the pitch of the string goes up a semitone.
2 The women next door kept me awake bawling at her husband half the night.

It's not very difficult to guess that a 'fret' is one of the thin pieces of metal that separate the notes on a guitar, or that 'bawling' must mean talking aggressively or shouting.

Some words can be guessed from looking at their form. For instance, you may never have seen 'untaxable' before, but the different parts of the word – un, tax, able – should each tell you something and help you to guess the meaning. What do you think 'pre-heated', 'over-sensitivity', 'antimilitarist', and 'incomprehensibility' mean? What kind of people do you think 'horsey' or 'bookish' people are?

Don't expect to be able to guess all the new words in a text. There will be some that you can only get a vague idea of, and a few will be impossible. Don't waste too much time worrying about these: the most important thing is to understand the text as a whole as well as possible, and one or two difficult words won't usually make much difference.

Exercise a

You probably don't know many of these words: famished, flipper, shred, trudge, lintel, gaudy, sallow, surreptitiously, goggle, pillion.

Look at the way they are used in the following sentences and then say, or write, what you think they might mean. (Don't use a dictionary, of course.)

1 Have you got a piece of bread or something? I'm absolutely famished.
2 'My God, he's swimming fast.' 'Yes, he's got flippers on.'
3 She read my letter slowly to the end and then tore it to shreds.

Teaching unit 2

4 On the way, we drove past a column of depressed-looking soldiers, trudging along wearily through the mud and rain.
5 The door was so low I hit my head on the lintel.
6 Sebastian hates fairs. The loud, vulgar music, the cheap gaudy colours, the noise, the whole atmosphere – everything makes him feel ill.
7 Twenty years in an unhealthy tropical climate had given his face a permanently sallow complexion.
8 I looked round the church: two of the children were playing cards under the seat, and another was surreptitiously eating a cream bun.
9 What are you all goggling at me like that for? Have I got two heads or something?
10 Mark got on the motorbike, I sat behind him on the pillion, and we roared off into the night.

Exercise b

Read the following text slowly and carefully without a dictionary, and without asking any questions. Then write down all the words and expressions in italics, and any others that you don't know. Look carefully at the context of each unknown word or expression, and write down what you think it might mean.

Baggy pants

Everyone laughed when Albert went to work in his *baggy pants*. Everyone but Albert. He punched one of his workmates in the eye.

And that's when the joke really *fell flat*. For the incident led to a strike which *crippled* production at a carpet factory.

The trousers that caused all the trouble were in a *shapeless fawn*-coloured material. They *flapped* round Albert's legs as he walked into the Victoria carpet factory in Kidderminster, Worcestershire.

Other workers *winked* and *smirked*. There were *ribald* comments. Albert thought it was quite amusing at first. But after half an hour, the *wisecracks got him down*.

So he *planted one on* seventeen-year-old apprentice David Bishop. Then the foreman *intervened*. He didn't see the funny side of it. He *suspended* David for two days and Albert for three.

Other workers held an emergency meeting and decided that David had been treated unfairly. They asked for him to be *reinstated*. The management refused – and 100 men walked out.

David said at home in Kidderminster yesterday: 'The trousers were just hopeless. You could have got two people in them. But it seems our fun went too far. Albert suddenly came across and hit me in the face. Later, the foreman sent me home. I have lost £3 in wages and that hurts me more than anything.'

The strikers are expected back at work today. But no one is expecting a return of Albert's troublesome trousers.
(From a report in the *Daily Mirror*)

Practice unit 2.1

Read each text carefully, without a dictionary, and then answer the questions that follow. While reading, pay special attention to the words that you don't know: look carefully at the context and see if you can get an idea of what they mean.

Driver escapes through car boot

Mr Peter Johnson, aged twenty-three, battled for half an hour to escape from his trapped car yesterday when it landed upside down in three feet of water. Mr Johnson took the only escape route – through the boot.

Mr Johnson's car had finished up in a dike at Romney Marsh, Kent, after skidding on ice and hitting a bank. 'Fortunately the water began to come in only slowly,' Mr Johnson said. 'I couldn't force the doors because they were jammed against the banks of the dike, and daren't open the windows because I knew water would come flooding in.'

Mr Johnson, a sweets salesman, of Holly Bank Hill, London Road, Sittingbourne, Kent, first tried to attract the attention of other motorists by sounding the horn and hammering on the roof and the boot. Then he began his struggle to escape.

Later he said: 'It was really a halfpenny which saved my life. It was the only coin I had in my pocket and I used it to unscrew the back seat to get into the boot. As I worked on the screws I could feel the water collecting underneath me on the roof. I hammered desperately with a wrench trying to make someone hear, but no help came.'

It took ten minutes to unscrew the seat – and a further five minutes to clear the sweet samples from the boot. Then, Mr Johnson found a wrench and began to work on the boot lock. Fifteen desperate minutes ebbed away. 'It was the only chance I had. Finally it gave but as soon as I moved the boot lid the water and mud gushed in. I forced the lid down into the mud and scrambled clear as the car filled up.'

His hands and arms cut and bruised, Mr Johnson got to Beckett Farm nearby where he was looked after by the farmer's wife, Mrs Lucy Bates. Huddled in a rug, he said: 'That thirty minutes seemed like hours.' Only the tips of the car wheels were visible, police said last night. The vehicle had sunk into two feet of mud at the bottom of the dike.
(From a report in *The Guardian*)

Exercise a

Here are nine words and expressions from the text. Each is followed by four explanations of its meaning: only one is correct. Write down the numbers of the words and expressions, followed by the letters of the correct definitions. (For example, if you think 'boot' means 'back window', write 1a.) Do this exercise without a dictionary.

1 *boot* (line 3)
a) back window
b) space for luggage at the back of the car
c) space for luggage at the front of the car
d) engine compartment

2 *dike* (line 4)
a) lake
b) small farm road

Practice unit 2.1

   c) channel full of water at the side of the road
   d) canal

3 *wrench* (line 14)
   a) a kind of tool
   b) a kind of box
   c) a bunch of keys
   d) one of the controls of the car

4 *samples* (line 16)
   a) boxes
   b) catalogues
   c) examples of what a salesman is trying to sell
   d) rubbish

5 *ebbed away* (line 17)
   a) were left
   b) were all he had
   c) went past very slowly
   d) were used up

6 *it gave* (line 17)
   a) it presented itself to me
   b) it came open
   c) I got something from it
   d) I stopped trying

7 *gushed* (line 18)
   a) poured
   b) came slowly
   c) made a loud noise
   d) felt cold

8 *huddled* (line 21)
   a) talking
   b) interviewed
   c) wrapped up warmly
   d) confused

9 *tips* (line 22)
   a) outside parts
   b) rubber parts
   c) metal parts
   d) tops

Pidgin English

There is a story of a British consul in China who was asked to marry a young Danish sailor and a Chinese girl – no one of the three knowing the other languages. Accordingly, the official said to the bride, 'This man wantchee take you home-side makee wife-pidgin. Can do, no can do?' Said she demurely, 'Can do', and the consul pronounced them man and wife.   5

Practice unit 2.1

Pidgin English, though sometimes ignored and derided as 'baby talk', is a legitimate, useful language that continues to gather converts. It is still the lingua franca of a large part of the Pacific Islands, and an estimated 30 to 50 million people speak some form of it, either solely or as an adjunct to their native tongues.

To be sure, its limited vocabulary can engender some laughable quotations, such as the description of a piano by a New Guinea native: 'Him fella big box, you fight him, he cry.' Or the classic announcement by a Chinese servant that his master's prize sow had given birth to a litter: 'Him cow pig have kittens.'

But pidgin's seemingly imprecise vocabulary can be almost poetic at times.

There could hardly be, in any language, a friendlier definition of a friend than the Australian aborigine's 'him brother belong me'. Or consider his description of the sun: 'lamp belong Jesus'. Pidgin can be forthright, too. An Aussie policeman is 'gubmint catchum-fella'. An elbow is 'screw belong arm'. Whiskers are 'grass belong face'. When a man is thirsty, 'him belly allatime burn'.

The English pidgin we know today was born on the China coast 300 years ago when the Western nations first began to trade there. The crews of merchant vessels were disinclined to learn Chinese, and the Chinese saw little sense in the involved grammatical locutions of the traders' languages. They compromised by adapting the Westerners' words to Chinese syntax. The resultant goulash became known as 'business' language, or because the closest a Chinese could come to pronouncing business was 'bishin' or 'bijin' – eventually pidgin. (It has nothing to do with a pigeon though it's sometimes spelt that way.)

Might pidgin some day become the one international 'earth language'?

Professor William Marquardt of New York University's linguistics department disabused me of that rosy notion. 'Although all the varieties of pidgin are alike in that they lack case, gender, tense and number,' he said, 'each form of pidgin must rely on the structural pattern of the native language to make sense.'

In the latter-day compulsion to 'civilize' every 'backward' nation in sight, pidgin is invariably considered by Western-world policy makers one of the first backwardnesses to be jettisoned. This could prove to be a mistake. Robert Hall, professor of linguistics at Cornell University, points out in his book, *Hands Off Pidgin English!*, that the New Guinea native can learn Melanesian pidgin well enough in six months to begin instruction as a medical assistant. To achieve a command of English sufficient to undertake the same instruction would require five or six years.

In 1953, a U.N. Trusteeship Council recommended – among other improvements – that the pidgin used in New Guinea's trust territory be abolished and gradually replaced by English. But the language appears to be here to stay, beyond the powers of prohibition. In July 1962, when the U.N. invited one of the native members of its Trusteeship Council – a prosperous copra planter named Somu Sigob – to address a meeting at the New York headquarters, he nonplussed the delegates by addressing them in pidgin.

(Abridged; from an article by Gary Jennings in *Reader's Digest*)

Exercise b

Choose the correct answer to each question (without using a dictionary).

1 What do you think the British consul's sentence (lines 3–4) means?
a) This man wants to marry you – do you want to marry him?
b) This man wants to know if you are married.

Practice unit 2.1

c) This man wants you to live with him in Denmark.
d) This man wants to marry you and take you to his country. Do you agree to that?

2 'Derided' (line 6) means
a) laughed at
b) mixed up
c) stupid
d) taught

3 What is an 'adjunct' (line 9)?
a) an explanation
b) something added
c) a dialect
d) an ungrammatical form

4 A 'litter' (line 13) is
a) a mess
b) waste paper
c) a baby pig
d) a family of baby animals

5 What do you think the pidgin English word 'gubmint' (line 17) means?
a) judgement
b) enjoyment
c) government
d) policeman

6 'Disinclined' (lines 21–2) means
a) willing
b) unable
c) unwilling
d) too busy

7 'Goulash' (line 24) means
a) a kind of food
b) a mixture of all sorts of things
c) dialect
d) pidgin English

8 What is meant by 'disabused me of that rosy notion' (lines 29–30)?
a) insulted me for having such a silly idea
b) showed me that my nice idea was impossible
c) agreed with my attractive idea
d) discussed my interesting idea politely

9 'Latter-day' (line 33) means
a) modern
b) old-fashioned
c) permanent
d) impossible

Practice unit 2.2

10 'Jettisoned' (line 35) means
a) thrown out
b) learnt
c) improved
d) criticised

11 What do you think 'nonplussed' means (line 45)?
a) made angry
b) pleased
c) insulted
d) surprised and confused

12 Pidgin is basically
a) a very bad kind of English.
b) a mixture of English, Chinese, Australian and Melanesian.
c) simplified Chinese.
d) a language containing mainly English-based words but using the grammatical system of another language.

13 Which of the following suggestions is not contained in the text?
a) Pidgin is spoken by a lot of people.
b) Some people can learn pidgin much more quickly than English.
c) Pidgin is an official language at the United Nations.
d) It is impossible to stop people speaking pidgin.

Practice unit 2.2

Read the text carefully, without a dictionary, and then answer the questions that follow. While reading, pay special attention to the words that you don't know: look carefully at the context and see if you can get an idea of what they mean.

Blue film

I slept until half past seven, when I got up and changed into my suit. I knew Spider would be wearing his best gear. I met him round the corner so as not to let the hotel staff see us together, and then we drove into Soho whistling from the Rolls at every good-looking bird we saw on the way.

Once a big bloke in a sports car caught me up and wanted to start an argument because he said I'd insulted his bird at the last lot of traffic lights, but I said, 'Couldn't have been me ducky, I can't whistle, and anyway us two are...that way dearie.' I gave a camp wave of the wrist.

He looked at us but then revved up and drove off like a maniac while Spider fell under the dashboard in convulsions. You could easily tell it was going to be a great night.

In Soho we stopped for a chinwag with two of Spider's cronies who were leaning against the wall outside a narrow entrance. There were a dozen or more signs naming enterprises that had failed upon that spot.

'It's a billiards room,' said Spider, 'fancy a game?'

'No thanks,' I said.

Two tourists came past. One of Spider's friends – a man called Newmarket Tony – spoke to them softly and respectfully. 'Like to see a blue film sir? Just about to start.' In his hand he had a book of numbered tickets.

'How much?'

'Five pounds for each of you gentlemen. Just about to start.'

'Make it three pounds each,' said one of the tourists. Newmarket Tony considered the matter but reluctantly declined. 'I'd like to do it,' he explained, 'but there's the projectionist to pay and the fellow that owns the place. I couldn't do it for less than four pounds ten, and that's losing half of my own ten bob.'

The two tourists bought tickets from Tony's friend, a tall boy with spectacles who said very little. The tourists went upstairs, 'Have a cup of coffee first', called Tony after them. 'He's just sorting out the reels.'

Three football fans gathered around Newmarket Tony by this time, realising that he was dealing in something illicit and delightful. He sold them each a ticket and within four minutes had disposed of tickets to an elderly man with a briefcase and two Chinese waiters. 'Look son', said a passerby to Tony. 'I want to see a special blue film. Got me?'

'Sure thing,' said Newmarket Tony. 'What do you want?'

'I saw it before in a hotel room in Miami,' said the man. 'I'm Canadian and I've searched around the world for that film.'

'I've got all kinds,' said Newmarket Tony.

'This is a coloured boy, wrestling in mud with a Chinese girl. It's in the deep south and there's no referee. Got me? Two Lascar seamen join in at the end of the film. That's the only blue film I'd be interested in seeing.'

Behind the Canadian, an Italian boy with an expensive camera around his neck was asking for a translation of the Canadian's request. Before Newmarket Tony could reply, the Canadian added, 'I remember now, there's one bit where they all dress up in policeman's uniform.'

Newmarket Tony thought for no more than a second or two, 'You almost stumped me there sir,' he said. He smiled, 'That one came in today.'

'It did?' said the Canadian. 'Say that's really something.'

'Pay for this first one,' said Tony, 'and I'll get him to put that on right after.' The Canadian was as pleased as punch. 'Is that so,' he said. 'Well you fellows really do pick them out.' He rubbed his hands gleefully and went upstairs. So did the Italian boy.

'No cameras,' said Newmarket Tony. 'One of our rules. Cameras must be left at the door here.' The Italian reluctantly handed Tony his camera.

Newmarket Tony looked at his watch. 'Will you tell the others, it starts in three minutes. He's putting a new lamp in, the last one's going a bit dim.' The Italian boy didn't understand too well but finally nodded.

'Let's scarper,' said Newmarket Tony's friend.

'Can't we see the blue film?' I asked.

'Is your mate crackers?' Newmarket Tony asked Spider. 'Let's split.'

'It's a billiards place,' said Spider to me. 'I told you, didn't I?'

Newmarket Tony said a brief goodnight and hurried down the road stuffing the camera into his pocket. His friend hurried after him.

'Let's go,' said Spider. 'Sometimes they're really mad when they come out. One night six Irishmen smashed the billiards hall to pieces.'

(From *Only When I Larf*, by Len Deighton)

Practice unit 2.2

Exercise a

Here are thirteen words and expressions from the text. Each is followed by four explanations of its meaning; only one is correct. Write down the numbers of the words and expressions, followed by the letters of the correct definitions. (For example, if you think 'gear' means 'hat', write 1a.) Don't use a dictionary.

1 *gear* (line 2)
a) hat
b) clothes
c) shoes
d) jacket

2 *bird* (line 4)
a) feathered creature that can fly
b) friend
c) face
d) girl

3 *camp* (line 7)
a) place for tents
b) effeminate, homosexual
c) angry
d) friendly

4 *revved up* (line 9)
a) accelerated the engine
b) put on a serious expression
c) sat up straight
d) looked up

5 *in convulsions* (line 10)
a) because he was feeling ill
b) in order to hide
c) laughing uncontrollably
d) in great pain

6 *chinwag* (line 11)
a) drink
b) game of billards
c) conversation
d) argument

7 *cronies* (line 11)
a) friends
b) old ladies
c) victims
d) relations

8 *blue film* (line 17)
a) colour film
b) cartoon film

Practice unit 2.2

c) horror film
d) sex film

9 *Got me?* (line 37)
a) Do you understand?
b) Can you help me?
c) Do you agree?
d) Have you got it for me?

10 *You almost stumped me there sir* (lines 43–4)
a) Be careful – you nearly stepped on my foot
b) Your request was almost too difficult for me
c) You almost made me angry
d) I had difficulty in understanding you

11 *scarper* (line 54)
a) go in
b) divide the money
c) close the door
d) run away

12 *crackers* (line 56)
a) tired
b) rich
c) nervous
d) crazy

13 *split* (line 56)
a) leave him
b) have a drink
c) go away
d) beat him up

Exercise b: Same or different?

1 The narrator (the person who tells the story) woke up at 7.30 a.m.
2 The narrator was driving a sports car.
3 The narrator and Spider pretended to be homosexual.
4 They made another driver angry by whistling at his girlfriend.
5 They met some of Spider's friends outside a pornographic cinema.
6 Newmarket Tony and his friend sold ten tickets.
7 The Canadian wanted to see a special film.
8 Newmarket Tony's friend says nothing at all during the story.
9 Tony stole the Italian's camera.

Practice unit 2.3

Read each text carefully, without a dictionary, and then answer the questions that follow. While reading, pay special attention to the words that you don't know: look carefully at the context and see if you can get an idea of what they mean.

The front tail

Bond had walked for only a few minutes when it suddenly occurred to him that he was being followed. There was no evidence for it except a slight tingling of the scalp and an extra awareness of the people near him, but he had faith in his sixth sense and he at once stopped in front of the shop window he was passing and looked casually back along 46th Street. Nothing but a lot of miscellaneous people moving slowly on the sidewalks, mostly on the same side as himself, the side that was sheltered from the sun. There was no sudden movement into a doorway, nobody casually wiping his face with a handkerchief to avoid recognition, nobody bending down to tie a shoelace.

   Bond examined the Swiss watches in his shop window and then turned and sauntered on. After a few yards he stopped again. Still nothing. He went on and turned right into the Avenue of the Americas, stopping in the first doorway, the entrance to a women's underwear store where a man in a tan suit with his back to him was examining the black lace pants on a particularly realistic dummy. Bond turned and leant against a pillar and gazed lazily but watchfully out into the street.

   And then something gripped his pistol arm and a voice snarled: 'All right, Limey. Take it easy unless you want lead for lunch,' and he felt something press into his back just above the kidneys.

   What was there familiar about that voice? The Law? The Gang? Bond glanced down to see what was holding his right arm. It was a steel hook. Well, if the man had only one arm! Like lightning he swivelled, bending sideways and bringing his left fist round in a flailing blow, low down.

   There was a smack as his fist was caught in the other man's left hand, and at the same time as the contact telegraphed to Bond's mind that there could have been no gun, there came the well-remembered laugh and the lazy voice saying: 'No good, James. The angels have got you.'

   Bond straightened himself slowly and for a moment he could only gaze into the grinning hawk-like face of Felix Leiter with blank disbelief, his built-up tension slowly relaxing.

   'So you were doing a front tail, you lousy bastard,' he finally said.

(From *Diamonds are Forever* by Ian Fleming)

Exercise a

Choose the correct answer to each question (without using a dictionary).

1 'Sixth sense' (line 3) means
a) instinct
b) common sense
c) sense of humour
d) memory

Practice unit 2.3

2 Why did Bond stop in the doorway to the underwear shop?
a) to look at the man in the tan suit
b) to look at the underwear
c) to get out of the heat
d) to see who was following him

3 What is a 'dummy' (line 13)?
a) a model used for displaying clothes
b) a beautiful girl
c) somebody who can't speak
d) an advertisement

4 What do you think 'snarled' means (line 15)?
a) laughed
b) said unpleasantly
c) whispered
d) asked

5 What is meant by 'Take it easy unless you want lead for lunch' (line 16)?
a) You go first slowly and we'll have lunch together.
b) Take the gun gently or it will go off.
c) Don't move or I'll shoot you.
d) Put your hands up.

6 'Swivelled' (line 20) means
a) said some bad words
b) dropped to the ground
c) turned quickly
d) jumped into the air

7 Bond knew that the other man had no gun (line 23) because
a) he was in contact with him.
b) he received a message.
c) he saw that the man's hand was empty.
d) he felt that the man's hand was empty.

8 What does 'doing a front tail' mean (line 29)?
a) walking backwards
b) 'following' somebody from in front
c) hiding behind people
d) pretending to be somebody else

Waiting for the lorry

The lorry had been ordered to arrive at the rest-house at seven-thirty for loading, and by eight-thirty we thought we should be well on the road. It was very apparent that we were new to Africa. At ten o'clock we were pacing round and round our mountain of luggage

Practice unit 2.3

on the veranda, cursing and fuming impotently, scanning the road for the truant lorry.
At eleven o'clock a cloud of dust appeared on the horizon and in its midst, like a beetle
in a whirlwind, was the lorry. It screeched to a halt below, and the driver dismounted.
I noticed an assortment of odd passengers sitting in the back, about twelve of them, chatting happily to each other with their goats, chickens, bags of yams, calabashes of palm
wine, and other necessities of travel spread out around them in the lorry. I stormed down
to interview the driver, and it was then I learned that it is better not to inquire why a
lorry is late in the Cameroons: I was treated to at least six different and contradictory
reasons, none of which satisfied anyone except the driver. Wisely leaving this subject,
I turned my attention to the crowd in the back of the vehicle. It transpired that this was
the driver's wife, this was the driver's wife's cousin, this was the father of the motor-boy,
and this was the motor-boy's mother-in-law, and so on. After a prolonged altercation
they were removed, together with their household goods and livestock. The driver then
had to turn the lorry for loading, and my faith in his abilities was rudely shattered when
he backed twice into the hibiscus hedge, and once into the rest-house wall. Our baggage
was then loaded with a speed and lack of care that was frightening, and, as I watched,
I wondered how much of our equipment would be left intact on arrival in Mamfe. I need
not have worried. It turned out later than only the most indispensable and irreplaceable
things got broken.
(By Gerald Durrell)

Exercise b

Here are some words and expressions from the text. Each is followed by four explanations
of its meaning; only one is correct. Write down the numbers of the words and expressions,
followed by the letters of the correct definitions. (For example, if you think 'pacing' means
'running', write 1a.) Do this exercise without a dictionary.

1 *pacing* (line 3)
a) running
b) walking impatiently
c) counting our steps
d) sitting

2 *fuming* (line 4)
a) angry
b) smoking
c) waiting
d) laughing

3 *scanning* (line 4)
a) walking along
b) standing beside
c) blaming
d) looking at every part of

4 *truant* (line 4)
a) that hadn't turned up
b) broken-down
c) old-fashioned
d) big

Practice unit 2.3

5 *screeched to a halt* (line 6)
a) crashed
b) stopped slowly
c) stopped with a loud noise
d) drove up to the door

6 *dismounted* (line 6)
a) got out
b) took the engine to pieces
c) opened the door
d) drove away again

7 *assortment* (line 7)
a) number
b) kind
c) varied collection
d) interesting group

8 *calabashes* (line 8)
a) gallons
b) containers
c) drinkers
d) very small bottles

9 *stormed* (line 9)
a) went very fast
b) went angrily
c) jumped
d) walked slowly

10 *transpired* (line 13)
a) was obvious
b) did not seem clear
c) was possible
d) became clear during the conversation

11 *altercation* (line 15)
a) drive
b) fight
c) rest
d) disagreement

12 *livestock* (line 16)
a) relations
b) necessities of travel
c) goats and chickens
d) important personal possessions

Section B:
Open-ended tests and summary-writing

Teaching unit 3: Open-ended tests

In units 1 and 2 the main task was reading and understanding. The questions were mostly recognition tests: all you had to do was to decide which answers were right. 'Open-ended' tests are a little more difficult; you not only have to understand the text and the questions – you also have to decide how to express the answer. They test composition as well as comprehension.

Using your own words

It's a good idea, when you answer questions like these, to use your own words as far as possible. Obviously you can't avoid using some words from the text - if the passage is about submarines, for example, it's difficult to write about it without using the word 'submarine' – but you should be careful not to use long expressions or whole sentences from the passage in your answers.

For example, imagine that a comprehension passage contains the sentence 'Many Americans are extremely reluctant to discuss the colour problem'. If you were asked 'What does the passage say about Americans' attitude to the colour problem?' it would not be a very good idea to write 'Many of them are extremely reluctant to discuss it'. This might make people feel that you hadn't really understood the text, or that you didn't know enough English to express the meaning in a different way. A much better answer would be 'Many of them are very unwilling to talk about it' or 'Many Americans strongly dislike talking about it'. (There are usually several possible ways to express an answer to this sort of question.)

Complete sentences

Write the answer in its most natural form, as you think an English person would express it. We don't always make complete sentences in answer to questions beginning with interrogative words like 'why', 'where' or 'what'.

Examples:
1   Question: *Where are penguins found?*
    Answer: *In the Antarctic.* (Not *Penguins are found in...*)
2   Question: *Why did you become a teacher?*
    Answer: *Because I wanted to feel superior.* (Not *I became a teacher because I...*)

Teaching unit 3

Pronouns etc.

In some questions, you will be asked to give the meaning of a word like 'it' or 'that', or to say what one of these words refers to in the passage.

Examples:
1. In the sentence 'He put the gun in the drawer, closed it, and took another one out of his pocket', what does 'it' refer to?
2. In the same sentence, what does 'one' mean?

These questions aren't usually difficult. You simply have to look at the context and put in your answer a word or expression which could be used instead of 'it', etc. The answer to the first question is 'the drawer', and the second answer is 'gun'.

Exercise

Read the text slowly and carefully, and then answer the questions that follow.

Trafalgar Square Rally

Phoebe Graham's all right, is he?
Jean Yes, he's all right.
Phoebe There's nothing wrong there, is there?
Billy Why don't you mind your bloody business? She'll tell you if she wants to.
Phoebe All right, I know. She doesn't mind telling me if there's anything, do you?   5
Jean We had a slight disagreement. Nothing more, that's all.
Phoebe After all, she may not be my own, but I did help to bring her up a little, didn't I? After all, she's Archie's daughter. Be a bit strange if I wasn't interested whether she was happy or not. Oh, well, dear, don't take any notice. You'll soon make it up. Men are funny. You don't want to take any notice of them.   10
Jean (*smiling*). Wish I didn't.
Phoebe That's right. Have another drink. You'll soon feel better. What did you have a row about? Something silly I'll bet. You haven't broken off your engagement?
Jean I don't know. Probably.
Phoebe Oh dear, I'm sorry.   15
Jean I went to the Rally in Trafalgar Square last Sunday.
Billy You did what?
Jean I went to the Rally in Trafalgar Square.
Billy What for, for God's sake?
Jean Because, Grandad, somehow – with a whole lot of other people, strange as it   20
may seem – I managed to get myself steamed up about the way things were going.
Billy And you went to Trafalgar Square?
Phoebe Well she said so didn't she?
Billy Well I should think you want your bloody head read!   25
Jean That was more or less Graham's feeling about it. Only he happens to be about fifty years younger than you, and he put it a bit differently. It all really started over something I wanted to do, and then it all came out, lots of things. All kinds of bitterness – things I didn't even know existed.
Billy I didn't know you were interested in politics.   30

Teaching unit 3

Jean   Neither did I. I've always found the whole thing rather boring.

Billy   Good God! I've heard some things in my time. This is what comes of giving them the bloody vote. They start breaking their engagements, just because they believe every shiftless lay-about writing for the papers.

Phoebe   Oh, shut up, just for a minute, Dad. You had a row because of something you wanted to do?

Jean   Well, it's – oh, it's a complicated story. I think I wrote and told you I was teaching Art to a bunch of Youth Club kids.

Phoebe   Oh, yes. That was ages ago.

Jean   Nearly a year. I knew someone who had been doing it – a young man Graham knew. He said it was too much for him, and he couldn't stick it any longer. 'They're little bastards the lot of them,' he said. 'If anyone believes you can teach those monsters to create anything, they're crazy. They're a lot of little bastards.' That's what he said. But – something, something, made me want to have a go at it. There wasn't any money in it. Just a few shillings for a few nights a week. But it was something I knew a little about – or thought I knew about. I'd never been good enough to paint myself, but I thought this was something I really could do. Even if it was just battling a gang of moronic teenagers. The Club leader thought I was mad, and so did Graham.

Phoebe   I can't say I blame him really. It doesn't sound a very nice job at all. Not for a young girl like you, Jean. They sound like a real tough crowd to me.

Jean   They were. Too tough for either of the young men who had taken them on before.

Phoebe   Well if they don't want to learn, why do they go for heaven's sake?

Jean   It was an obligatory class, if they attended one of my classes a week, they could take part in the Club's other activities – the dances and so on. I fought those kids back – and some of them were eight feet tall. Most of the time I've loathed it, and I loathed them. I pretended to myself that I didn't, but I did. I hated them, but I think I was getting somewhere. And now Graham wants me to marry him. Now, before he's qualified but I wouldn't. He doesn't want me to try something for myself. He doesn't want me to threaten him or his world, he doesn't want me to succeed. I refused him. Then it all came out – Trafalgar Square and everything. You know, I hadn't realized – it just hadn't occurred to me that you could love somebody, that you could want them, and want them twenty-four hours of the day and then suddenly find that you're neither of you even living in the same world. I don't understand that. I just don't understand it. I wish I could understand it. It's frightening. Sorry, Phoebe, I shouldn't be drinking your gin. I bought this for you.

(From *The Entertainer* by John Osborne)

1. What is Graham's relationship to Jean?
2. What is the relationship between Billy and Jean?
3. What is the relationship between Phoebe and Billy?
4. What is the relationship between Phoebe and Jean?
5. What is Billy's attitude to the Rally in Trafalgar Square?
6. What was the purpose of the Rally?
7. What did Graham feel about Jean going to the Rally?
8. Why did the 'Youth Club kids' go to Jean's Art class?
9. Why does Graham want to marry Jean at once?

Practice unit 3.1

10 Why did Jean's visit to Trafalgar Square start a quarrel between her and Graham?
11 What does Phoebe mean by 'she may not be my own' (line 7)?
12 Explain 'I managed to get myself steamed up about the way things were going' (lines 21–2).
13 Explain the meaning of 'Well I should think you want your bloody head read' (line 25)
14 What is 'it' in 'he put it a bit differently' (line 27)?
15 What is 'it' in 'It all really started' (line 27)?
16 Who are 'them' in line 33?
17 Who or what are 'those monsters' (line 43)?
18 What does 'it' mean in 'it was something I knew a little about' (line 46)?
19 'It all came out' (line 62). What all came out?
20 What does Jean mean when she says 'you're neither of you even living in the same world' (lines 65–6)?
21 What is 'this' in line 67?

Practice unit 3.1

Read the following text slowly and carefully and then answer the questions.

The reconciliation

'I came round because I really think the whole thing is too absurd.'
　'So do I. I always did.'
　'You can't have half as much as I did. I mean really, when one comes to think of it. And after all these years.'
　'Oh, I know. And I dare say if you hadn't, I should have myself. I'm sure the last thing 5
I want is to go on like this. Because really, it's too absurd.'
　'That's what I think. Is it all right, then?'
　'Absolutely, as far as I'm concerned. What I mean is, I never have believed in keeping things up. I'm not that kind of person.'
　'Neither am I, for that matter.' 10
　'Oh no, dear, I know. But I must say, you took the whole thing up exactly in the way I *didn't* mean it, in a way. Not that it matters now.'
　'Well, it's all over now, but, to be absolutely honest, I must say I can't quite see how anybody could possibly have taken it any other way. Not really, I mean.'
　'Well, you said that I said every one said you were spoiling the child, and of course, 15
what I really said wasn't that at all.'
　'Well, dear, you say that now, I know, but what you said at the *time* was exactly what I said you said. Or so it seemed to me.'
　'Well, there's not much object in going over the whole thing all over again now it's over, is there? But if you'd come straight to me at the time, I must say I think it would 20
all have been simpler. It doesn't *matter*, of course, now it's all over and done with, but I just think it would have been simpler, that's all.'
　'Still, dear, it's perfectly simple as it is, isn't it? If you think I spoil the child, you're quite entitled to your own opinion, naturally. All I said was, that it seemed a pity to tell everybody that everybody thought so, when really it was just simply what *you* thought. And 25

Practice unit 3.1

I must say, I can't help being rather amused, but we all know that lookers-on see most of the game – it just *amuses* me, that's all.'

'Very well, dear, if you choose to be offended you must *be* offended, that's all. As I said at the time, and *still* say, no one is fonder of children than I am, but to let any child go to rack and ruin for want of one single word seems to me a pity, that's all. Just a pity.' 30

'Have it your own way, dear. I shouldn't dream of contradicting you. Actually, it was only the other day that someone was saying how extraordinarily well brought up the child seemed to be, but I dare say that's got nothing to do with it whatever.'

'Well, all I've got to say is that it's a pity.'

'And if there's one thing I'm *not*, it's ready to take offence. I never have been, and I 35 never shall be.'

'Besides, while we're on the subject, I don't understand about the blue wool, and I never shall understand.'

'We've gone over the whole of the blue wool at least twenty times already.'

'I dare say, and I'm not saying anything at all. In fact, I'd rather not.' 40

'And if it comes to that, I may not have said very much about it – it's not my way – but it would be an absolute lie if I said that I didn't remember all that fuss about the library books.'

'I said at the time, and I still say, that the library books were a storm in a tea-cup.'

'Very well, dear. Nobody wants to quarrel less than I do.' 45

'As I always say, it takes two to make a quarrel. Besides, it's so absurd.'

'That's what I say. Why be so absurd as to quarrel, is what I say. Let bygones be bygones. The library books are *over* now, and that's all about it.'

'It's like the blue wool. When a thing is over, let it *be* over, is what I always say. I don't want to say anything more about anything at all. The only thing I must say is that when 50 you say I said that everybody said that about your spoiling that child, it simply isn't what I said. That's all. And I don't want to say another word about it.'

'Well, certainly I don't. There's only one thing I simply can't help saying...'
(From an extract by E. M. Delafield in *Modern Humour*)

Exercise

1. What is the purpose of the first speaker in calling on the second?
2. Explain briefly what they seem to have quarrelled about in the past.
3. Do you feel that one of the two is more quarrelsome than the other, or are they more or less the same?
4. What is 'the whole thing' (line 1)?
5. What does the first speaker mean by 'And after all these years' (lines 3–4)?
6. What is meant by 'Is it all right, then?' (line 7)?
7. What was 'exactly what I said you said' (lines 17–18)?
8. What is meant by 'We've gone over the whole of the blue wool' (line 39)?
9. Rewrite the following expressions so as to give the same meaning in different words:
   —to go on like this (line 6)
   —keeping things up (lines 8–9)
   —taken it any other way (line 14)
   —lookers-on see most of the game (lines 26–7)
   —to let any child go to rack and ruin for lack of one single word (lines 29–30)
   —Have it your own way (line 31)
10. The sentence 'I always did' (line 2) could be rewritten in more complete form as 'I

always did think (or 'I always thought') the whole thing was too absurd.' Rewrite the following sentences in the same way so as to make their meanings completely clear:
—You can't have half as much as I did (line 3)
—If you hadn't, I should have myself (line 5)
—I never have been, and I never shall be (lines 35–6)
—I'd rather not (line 40)

11 Explain the meaning of the word 'it' in
—'I may not have said very much about it' (line 41)
—'it's not my way' (line 41)
—'it's so absurd' (line 46)
—'It's like the blue wool' (line 49)

Practice unit 3.2

Read the following text slowly and carefully and then answer the questions.

The pistol

But first he had to get it, damn it all!

He had gone almost all the way forward when he saw the first one, up here, that somebody was not wearing. Doll stopped and stared at it hungrily, before he bethought himself to look around at the situation. The pistol hung from the end of a bed frame. Three bunks away in the heat a group of men clustered around a nervous crapgame. In the companionway itself four or five other men stood talking about fifteen feet away. All in all, it was certainly not any less risky than the two he'd seen in the stern. Perhaps it was even a little more so.

On the other hand, Doll could not forget the maddening sense of time running out. This might be the only one he would see up here. After all, he had only seen two in the entire stern. In desperation he decided he had better chance it. No one was taking any notice of him as far as he could tell. Casually, Doll stepped over and leaned on the bunk frame for a moment, as if he belonged here, then lifted the pistol off and buckled it around his waist. Stifling his instinct to just up and run, he lit a cigarette and took a couple of deep drags, then started leisurely towards the door, back the way he had come.

He had gotten halfway to it, and, indeed, had begun to think that he had pulled it off, when he heard the two voices hollering behind him. There was no doubt they were aimed at him.

'Hey, you!'

'Hey, soldier!'

Doll turned, able to feel his eyes getting deep and guilty-looking as his heart began to beat more heavily, and saw two men, one a private and one a sergeant, coming down toward him. Would they turn him in? Would they try to beat him up? Neither of these prospects bothered Doll half so much as the prospect of being treated with contempt like the sneak-thief he felt he was. That was what Doll was afraid of: It was like one of those nightmares everybody has of getting caught, but does not believe will ever really happen to them.

Practice unit 3.2

The two men came on down toward Doll ominously, looking indignant, their faces dark with outraged righteousness. Doll blinked his eyes rapidly several times, trying to wash from them the self-conscious guilt he could feel was in them. Behind the two, other faces had turned to watch, he noticed.

'That's my pistol you're wearin', soldier,' the private said. His voice held injured accusation.

Doll said nothing.

'He saw you take it off the bunk,' the sergeant said. 'So don't try to lie out of it, soldier.'

Summoning all his energy – or courage, or whatever it was – Doll still did not answer, and forced a slow, cynical grin to spread across his face, while he stared at them, unblinking now. Slowly he undid the belt and passed it over. 'How long you been in the army, mack?' he grinned. 'You oughta know fucking better than to leave your gear lyin' around like that. You might lose it someday.' He continued to stare, unflinching.

Both men stared back at him, their eyes widening slightly as the new idea, new attitude, replaced their own of righteous indignation. Indifference and cheerful lack of guilt made them appear foolish; and both men suddenly grinned sheepishly, penetrated as they had been by the fiction beloved in all armies of the tough, scrounging, cynical soldier who collects whatever he can get his hands on.

'Well, you better not have such sticky fingers, soldier,' the sergeant said, but it no longer carried much punch. He was trying to stifle his grin.

'Anything layin' around out in the open that loose, is fair game to me,' Doll said cheerfully. 'And to any other old soldier. Tell your boy he oughtn't to tempt people so much.'

Behind the two, the other faces had begun to grin too, at the private's discomfiture. The private himself had a hangdog look, as if he were the one at fault. The sergeant turned to him.

'Hear that, Drake?' he grinned. 'You better take better care of your fucking gear.'

'Yeah. He sure better,' Doll said. 'Or he won't have it very goddam long.' He turned and went on leisurely toward the door, and nobody tried to stop him.

(From *The Thin Red Line* by James Jones)

Exercise

1. What is 'it' in 'he had to get it' (line 1)?
2. 'He saw the first one' (line 2). The first what?
3. In 'it was certainly not any less risky' (line 7), what does 'it' refer to?
4. Why was it risky?
5. Why did Doll decide to take this pistol although it was dangerous?
6. Why did he walk leisurely (line 15)?
7. What is 'it' in 'halfway to it' (line 16)?
8. Explain the meaning of 'pulled it off' (line 16).
9. What do you think 'turn him in' means (line 23)?
10. When the two soldiers shouted after Doll, what was he most worried about?
11. Rewrite in a different way the expression 'Don't try to lie out of it' (line 34).
12. What do you think 'gear' means, in line 38?
13. What does 'collects' mean, in line 44?
14. Explain what Doll means by saying 'Anything layin' around out in the open that loose, is fair game to me' (line 47).
15. Explain in your own words why the two soldiers changed their attitude to Doll. (Answer in not more than 30 words.)

Practice unit 3.3

Read the following text slowly and carefully and then answer the questions.

Snowball and Napoleon

In January there came bitterly hard weather. The earth was like iron, and nothing could be done in the fields. Many meetings were held in the big barn, and the pigs occupied themselves with planning out the work of the coming season. It had come to be accepted that the pigs, who were manifestly cleverer than the other animals, should decide all questions of farm policy, though their decisions had to be ratified by a majority vote. This arrangement would have worked well enough if it had not been for the disputes between Snowball and Napoleon. These two disagreed at every point where disagreement was possible. If one of them suggested sowing a bigger acreage with barley, the other was certain to demand a bigger acreage of oats, and if one of them said that such and such a field was just right for cabbages, the other would declare that it was useless for anything except roots. Each had his own following, and there were some violent debates. At the Meetings Snowball often won over the majority by his brilliant speeches, but Napoleon was better at canvassing support for himself in between times. He was especially successful with the sheep. Of late the sheep had taken to bleating 'Four legs good, two legs bad' both in and out of season, and they often interrupted the Meeting with this. It was noticed that they were especially liable to break into 'Four legs good, two legs bad' at the crucial moments in Snowball's speeches. Snowball had made a close study of some back numbers of the *Farmer and Stockbreeder* which he had found in the farmhouse, and was full of plans for innovations and improvements. He talked learnedly about field-drains, silage, and basic slag, and had worked out a complicated scheme for all the animals to drop their dung directly in the fields, at a different spot every day, to save the labour of cartage. Napoleon produced no schemes of his own, but said quietly that Snowball's would come to nothing, and seemed to be biding his time. But of all their controversies, none was so bitter as the one that took place over the windmill.

In the long pasture, not far from the farm buildings, there was a small knoll which was the highest point on the farm. After surveying the ground, Snowball declared that this was just the place for a windmill, which could be made to operate a dynamo and supply the farm with electrical power. This would light the stalls and warm them in winter, and would also run a circular saw, a chaff-cutter, a mangel-slicer, and an electric milking machine. The animals had never heard of anything of this kind before (for the farm was an old-fashioned one and had only the most primitive machinery), and they listened in astonishment while Snowball conjured up pictures of fantastic machines which would do their work for them while they grazed at their ease in the fields or improved their minds with reading and conversation.

Within a few weeks Snowball's plans for the windmill were fully worked out. The mechanical details came mostly from three books which had belonged to Mr Jones – *One Thousand Useful Things to Do About the House*, *Every Man His Own Bricklayer*, and *Electricity for Beginners*. Snowball used as his study a shed which had once been used for incubators and had a smooth wooden floor, suitable for drawing on. He was closeted there for hours at a time. With his books held open by a stone, and with a piece of chalk gripped between the knuckles of his trotter, he would move rapidly to and fro, drawing in line after line and uttering little whimpers of excitement. Gradually the plans grew into a complicated mass of cranks and cog-wheels, covering more than half the floor,

Practice unit 3.3

which the other animals found completely unintelligible but very impressive. All of them came to look at Snowball's drawings at least once a day. Even the hens and ducks came, and were at pains not to tread on the chalk marks. Only Napoleon held aloof. He had declared himself against the windmill from the start. One day, however, he arrived unexpectedly to examine the plans. He walked heavily round the shed, looked closely at every detail of the plans and snuffed at them once or twice, then stood for a little while contemplating them out of the corner of his eye; then suddenly he lifted his leg, urinated over the plans, and walked out without uttering a word.

   The whole farm was deeply divided on the subject of the windmill. Snowball did not deny that to build it would be a difficult business. Stone would have to be quarried and built up into walls, then the sails would have to be made and after that there would be need for dynamos and cables. (How these were to be procured, Snowball did not say.) But he maintained that it could all be done in a year. And thereafter, he declared, so much labour would be saved that the animals would only need to work three days a week. Napoleon, on the other hand, argued that the great need of the moment was to increase food production, and that if they wasted time on the windmill they would all starve to death. The animals formed themselves into two factions under the slogans, 'Vote for Snowball and the three-day week' and 'Vote for Napoleon and the full manger'. Benjamin was the only animal who did not side with either faction. He refused to believe either that food would become more plentiful or that the windmill would save work. Windmill or no windmill, he said, life would go on as it had always gone on – that is, badly.
(From *Animal Farm* by George Orwell)

Exercise

1. What does the word 'their', in line 5, refer to?
2. What was 'this arrangement' (line 6)?
3. In the expression 'it was useless' (line 10), what does 'it' refer to?
4. What does 'each' mean, in line 11?
5. What do you think is meant by 'canvassing support' (line 13)?
6. Explain 'both in and out of season' (line 15).
7. What is 'this' in line 15?
8. What is meant by 'to break into' (line 16)?
9. Why did the sheep bleat at the crucial moments in Snowball's speeches?
10. What do you think is meant by 'back numbers' (line 17)?
11. What do you think the *Farmer and Stockbreeder* (line 18) was?
12. Explain in your own words what 'cartage' means (line 21).
13. What is meant by 'Snowball's' in line 22?
14. In 'this was just the place' (lines 26–7), what does 'this' refer to?
15. And what does 'this' refer to in 'this would light the stalls' (line 28)?
16. What is the subject of the verb 'would also run' in line 29?
17. What is the meaning of 'it' in 'it could all be done in a year' (line 56)?
18. In your own words, explain what advantages Snowball's schemes might bring to the animals.
19. Compare briefly (in not more than two sentences) Snowball's and Napoleon's attitudes to the economy of the farm.
20. Sum up Benjamin's attitude in not more than ten words.

Teaching unit 4: Introduction to summary

In comprehension tests, you are often asked to summarise a passage – to give the main ideas in a short paragraph of perhaps 100 words. This is particularly difficult to do when the passage is written in a complicated way, with long sentences or a lot of unusual vocabulary. You need to 'see through' the words to the ideas (often very simple) which lie behind them.

The following exercises will give you practice in doing this.

Exercise a

Each of these sentences can be rewritten much more briefly without really changing the meaning. Read them carefully, and then rewrite them in as few words as possible (between two and ten).

1 If I were asked to give an accurate description of my physical condition at the present moment, the only possible honest reply would be that I am greatly in need of liquid refreshment.
2 People whose professional activity lies in the field of politics are not, on the whole, conspicuous for their respect for factual accuracy.
3 I must confess to a feeling of very considerable affection for the young female person with whom I spend the greater part of my spare time.
4 Failure to assimilate an adequate quantity of solid food over an extended period of time is absolutely certain to lead, in due course, to a fatal conclusion.
5 It is by no means easy to achieve an accurate understanding of that subject of study which is concerned with the relationships between numbers.
6 It is my fervent wish that the creator of the universe will do his utmost to preserve and protect the royal lady who graciously occupies the position of head of state.
7 I should be greatly obliged if you would have the kindness to bring me, at your convenience, a written statement of the indebtedness I have incurred in connection with the meal which you have just finished serving to me.
8 The climatic conditions prevailing in the British Isles show a pattern of alternating and unpredictable periods of dry and wet weather, accompanied by a similarly irregular cycle of temperature changes.
9 I should be grateful if you would be so good as to stop the uninterrupted flow of senseless remarks with which you are currently straining my patience to breaking point.

Exercise b

Read these texts carefully and answer the questions that follow them.

Just leave the keys in, sir

Stan Murch, in a uniform-like blue jacket, stood on the sidewalk in front of the Hilton and watched cab after cab make the loop in to the main entrance. Doesn't anybody travel in their own car any more? Then at last a Chrysler Imperial with Michigan plates came hesitantly up Sixth Avenue, made the left-hand loop into the Hilton driveway and stopped at the entrance. As a woman and several children got out of the doors on the right of the car, toward the hotel entrance, the driver climbed heavily out on the left. He was a big man with a cigar and a camel's-hair coat.

  Murch was at the door before it was halfway open, pulling it the rest of the way and saying, 'Just leave the keys in it, sir.'

  'Right,' the man said around his cigar. He got out and sort of shook himself inside the coat. Then, as Murch was about to get behind the wheel, the driver said, 'Wait.'

  Murch looked at him. 'Sir?'

  'Here you go, boy,' the man said and pulled a folded dollar bill from his pants pocket and handed it across.

  'Thank you, sir,' Murch said. He saluted with the hand holding the dollar, climbed behind the wheel, and drove away. He was smiling as he made the right turn into 53rd Street; it wasn't every day a man gave you a tip for stealing his car.
(From *Bank Shot* by Donald E. Westlake)

Explain simply, in as few words as possible, exactly how Stan Murch got hold of a car.

Encounter groups

Because of the unstructured nature of the group, the major problem faced by the participants is how they are going to use their time together – whether it be eighteen hours of a week-end or forty or more hours in a one-week group. Often there is consternation, anxiety, and irritation at first – particularly because of the lack of structure. Only gradually does it become evident that the major aim of nearly every member is to find ways of relating to other members of the group and to himself. Then as they gradually, tentatively, and fearfully explore their feelings and attitudes towards one another and towards themselves, it becomes increasingly evident that what they have first presented are façades, masks. Only cautiously do the real feelings and real persons emerge. The contrast between the outer shell and the inner person becomes more and more apparent as the hours go by. Little by little, a sense of genuine communication builds up, and the person who has been thoroughly walled off from others comes out with some small segment of his actual feelings. Usually his attitude has been that his real feelings will be quite unacceptable to other members of the group. To his astonishment, he finds that he is more accepted the more real that he becomes. Negative feelings are often especially feared, since it seems certain to each individual that his angry or jealous feelings cannot possibly be accepted by another. Thus one of the most common developments is that a sense of trust slowly begins to build, and also a sense of warmth and liking for other members of the group. A woman says on Sunday afternoon, 'If anybody had told me Friday evening that by today I would be loving every member of this group I would have told him that he belonged in the nut house.' Participants feel a closeness and intimacy which they have not felt even with their spouses or members of their own family, because they have revealed themselves here more deeply and more fully than to those in their own family circle.

Thus, in such a group the individual comes to know himself and each of the others more completely than is possible in the usual social or working relationships. He becomes deeply acquainted with the other members and with his own inner self, the self that otherwise tends to be hidden behind his façade. Hence he relates better to others, both in the group and later in the everyday life situation.
(From *Encounter Groups* by Carl Rogers)

Explain in one short sentence what happens to people who take part in encounter groups, according to the passage.

Fictions

Doll had learned something during the past six months of his life. Chiefly what he had learned was that everybody lived by a selected fiction. Nobody was really what he pretended to be. It was as if everybody made up a fiction story about himself, and then he just pretended to everybody that that was what he was. And everybody believed him, or at least accepted his fiction story. Doll did not know if everybody learned this about life when they reached a certain age, but he suspected that they did. They just didn't tell it to anybody. And rightly so. Obviously, if they told anybody, then their own fiction story about themselves wouldn't be true either. So everybody *had* to learn it for himself. And then, of course, pretend he hadn't learned it.

Doll's own first experience of this phenomenon had come from, or at least begun with, a fist fight he had had six months ago with one of the biggest, toughest men in C-for-Charlie: Corporal Jenks. They had fought each other to a standstill, because neither would give up, until finally it was called a sort of draw-by-exhaustion. But it wasn't this so much as it was the sudden realisation that Corporal Jenks was just as nervous about having the fight as he was, and did not really want to fight any more than he did, which had suddenly opened Doll's eyes. Once he'd seen it here, in Jenks, he began to see it everywhere, in everybody.

When Doll was younger, he had believed everything everybody told him about themselves. And not only told him – because more often than not they didn't tell you, they just showed you. Just sort of let you see it by their actions. They acted what they wanted you to think they were, just as if it was really what they really were. When Doll had used to see someone who was brave and a sort of hero, he, Doll, had really believed he was that. And of course this made him, Doll, feel cheap because he knew he himself could never be like that. Christ, no wonder he had taken a back seat all his life!

It was strange, but it was as if you were honest and admitted you didn't know what you really were, or even if you were anything at all, then nobody liked you and you made everybody uncomfortable and they didn't want to be around you. But when you made up your fiction story about yourself and what a great guy you were, and then pretended that that was really you, everybody accepted it and believed you.
(From *The Thin Red Line* by James Jones)

Explain simply (in one sentence if possible) what was the important discovery Doll had made about the way people behave.

Practice unit 4.1

Read the text slowly and carefully, and then answer the questions that follow.

School and life

In my experience the problem of what to do in life was not made any easier by those who were entrusted with my education. Looking back, it seems most odd that never once in all the years that I was at school was there any general discussion about careers. As presumably the main object of going to school is to prepare for after life, it surely would have been very easy and relevant to organise lectures or discussions designed to give boys a broad view of the enormous variety of occupations open to men of average intelligence? Of course many boys were destined from birth to follow their fathers' careers, but even these would have benefited by glimpse of a wider horizon. Often and often in after life I have come across people doing jobs that I had never dreamed of before, and which would have thrilled me had I been told about them at school. I suppose the reason for this extraordinary omission is that so many schoolmasters had themselves such a restricted view. Spending all their time working to a rigid curriculum, the passing of examinations by their pupils gradually became the whole object of their working life. I recognize the importance of being made to learn things that one does not like, but surely it was not good to give the young mind the impression that all education was a form of mental gymnastics. For example, I used to find geometry rather fun, and, when I still had the naïve idea that what I was being taught might have some practical value, I asked what geometry was for. The only answer I ever got was that it taught one how to solve problems. If, instead, I had been told the simple fact that the word was derived from the Greek *ge*, the earth, and *metron*, a measure, and that the meaningless triangles that I was asked to juggle with formed the basis of geographical exploration, astronomy and navigation, the subject would immediately have assumed a thrilling romance, and, what is more, it would have been directly connected in my mind with the things that most appealed to me.

   My experience in this connection may have been unfortunate, but it was by no means unique; many of my friends who went to different schools confess to a similar experience, and complain that when they had completed their school education they had not the remotest idea of what they wanted to do. Moreover I do not think that this curiously detached attitude towards education was confined to schools. It had been intended that I should go to one of the great universities. I was tepid about the idea myself, for I had developed a dislike for the very thought of educational establishments. However, the prospect of three extra seasons in the Alps was a considerable incentive, and by dint of an enormous mental effort I succeeded in cramming sufficient Latin into my head to pass (at my second attempt) the necessary entrance examination. In due course I went to be interviewed by the master of my prospective college. When I was asked what subject I proposed to take when I came up to the university, I replied, somewhat diffidently, that I wanted to take Geology – diffidently, because I still regarded such things as having no reality in the hard world of work. The answer to my suggestion confirmed my fears. 'What on earth do you want to do with Geology? There is no opening there unless you eventually get a first and become a lecturer in the subject.' A *first*, a *lecturer* – I, who could not even learn a couple of books of Horace by heart! I felt that I was being laughed at. In fact I am sure I was not, and that my adviser was quite sincere and only trying to be helpful, but I certainly did not feel like arguing the matter. I listened meekly to suggestions that I should take Classics or Law, and left the room in a state of profound depression. 'Oh Lord,' I

Practice unit 4.2

thought, 'even here I won't be able to escape from Kennedy's Latin Primer,' with which I had been struggling for ten years. 45
(From *Upon That Mountain* by Eric Shipton)

Exercise

1. Sum up in one sentence the author's feeling about the value of his education.
2. What, in general, did his school fail to do?
3. Rewrite the first sentence of the text in your own words.
4. In what ways could his school have helped him more?
5. What sort of attitude did the teachers have towards education?
6. Why did he want to go to university?
7. Why did he decide not to go after all?
8. What was he really interested in?
9. Rewrite the sentence 'even these would have benefited by glimpses of a wider horizon' (lines 7–8) so as to show the meaning clearly.
10. In the expression 'I had been told about them' (line 10), what does 'them' refer to?
11. What was 'this extraordinary omission' (lines 10–11)?
12. In the expression 'their working life' (line 13), who or what does 'their' refer to?
13. What was 'the word' in line 19?
14. Explain what is meant by 'this curiously detached attitude towards education' (lines 27–8).
15. What do you think the author means by 'the prospect of three extra seasons in the Alps' (lines 30–1)?
16. Rewrite in simpler words 'by dint of an enormous mental effort' (lines 31–2).
17. 'The necessary entrance examination' (line 33). Necessary for what?
18. Why was the author shy about admitting that he wanted to study geology?
19. In the expression 'there is no opening there' (line 38), what does the second 'there' refer to?
20. Who was 'my adviser' (line 41)?

Practice unit 4.2

Read the text slowly and carefully, and then answer the questions that follow.

The eternal flaming racket of the female

Jimmy (*Turning to Cliff.*) She's so clumsy. I watch for her to do the same things every night. The way she jumps on the bed, as if she were stamping on someone's face, and draws the curtains back with a great clatter, in that casually destructive way of hers. It's like someone launching a battleship. Have you ever noticed how noisy women are? (*Crosses below chairs to L.C.*) Have you? The way they kick 5 the floor about, simply walking over it? Or have you watched them sitting at their dressing tables, dropping their weapons and banging down their bits of boxes and brushes and lipsticks?
He faces her dressing table.

Practice unit 4.2

I've watched her doing it night after night. When you see a woman in front of her bedroom mirror, you realise what a refined sort of a butcher she is. (*Turns in.*) Thank God they don't have many women surgeons! Those primitive hands would have your guts out in no time. Flip! Out it comes, like the powder out of its box. Flop! Back it goes, like the powder puff on the table.

Cliff (*grimacing cheerfully*). Ugh! Stop it!

Jimmy (*moving upstage*). She'd drop your guts like hair clips and fluff all over the floor. You've got to be fundamentally insensitive to be as noisy and as clumsy as that.
He moves C., and leans against the table.
I had a flat underneath a couple of girls once. You heard every damned thing those bastards did, all day and night. The most simple, everyday actions were a sort of assault course on your sensibilities. I used to plead with them. I even got to screaming the most ingenious obscenities I could think of, up the stairs at them. But nothing, nothing, would move them. With those two, even a simple visit to the lavatory sounded like a medieval siege. Oh, they beat me in the end – I had to go. I expect they're still at it. Or they're probably married by now, and driving some other poor devils out of their minds. Slamming their doors, stamping their high heels, banging their irons and saucepans – the eternal flaming racket of the female.
Church bells start ringing outside.

Jimmy Oh, hell! Now the bloody bells have started!
He rushes to the window.
Wrap it up, will you? Stop ringing those bells! There's somebody going crazy in here! I don't want to hear them!

Alison Stop shouting! (*Recovering immediately.*) You'll have Miss Drury up here.

Jimmy I don't give a damn about Miss Drury – that mild old gentlewoman doesn't fool me, even if she takes in you two. She's an old robber. She gets more than enough out of us for this place every week. Anyway, she's probably in church, (*points to the window*) swinging on those bloody bells!
Cliff goes to the window, and closes it.

Cliff Come on now, be a good boy. I'll take us all out, and we'll have a drink.

Jimmy They're not open yet. It's Sunday. Remember?
Anyway, it's raining.

Cliff Well, shall we dance?
He pushes Jimmy round the floor, who is past the mood for this kind of fooling.
Do you come here often?

Jimmy Only in the mating season. All right, all right, very funny.
He tries to escape, but Cliff holds him like a vice.
Let me go.

Cliff Not until you've apologised for being nasty to everyone. Do you think bosoms will be in or out, this year?

Jimmy Your teeth will be out in a minute, if you don't let go!
He makes a great effort to wrench himself free, but Cliff hangs on. They collapse to the floor C., below the table, struggling. Alison carries on with her ironing. This is routine, but she is getting close to breaking point, all the same. Cliff manages to break away, and finds himself in front of the ironing board. Jimmy springs up. They grapple.

Alison Look out, for heaven's sake! Oh, it's more like a zoo every day!
Jimmy makes a frantic, deliberate effort, and manages to push Cliff on to the ironing board, and into Alison. The board collapses. Cliff falls against her, and they end up in

Practice unit 4.3

a heap on the floor. Alison cries out in pain. Jimmy looks down at them, dazed and breathless. 60

Cliff (*picking himself up*). She's hurt. Are you all right?
Alison Well, does it look like it!
Cliff She's burnt her arm on the iron.
Jimmy Darling, I'm sorry.
Alison Get out! 65
Jimmy I'm sorry, believe me. You think I did it on pur——
Alison (*her head shaking helplessly*). Clear out of my *sight*!

He stares at her uncertainly. Cliff nods to him, and he turns and goes out of the door.
(From *Look Back in Anger* by John Osborne)

Exercise

1 Sum up very briefly (in three or four sentences) what happens in the scene.
2 What does Jimmy say about women? (Answer in one short sentence.)
3 What does he mean by 'their weapons' (line 7)?
4 Who is 'her' in line 10?
5 When Jimmy talks about 'those primitive hands' (line 12), which hands does he mean?
6 What is 'it' in 'out it comes' (line 13)?
7 Who is 'you' in line 19?
8 In the expression 'nothing would move them' (line 23), who is 'them'?
9 What does he mean by saying 'I expect they're still at it' (line 25)?
10 Rewrite in other words 'driving some other poor devils out of their minds' (line 26).
11 What does 'wrap it up' mean (line 32)?
12 Who do you think Miss Drury is?
13 What does the writer mean by 'this is routine' (line 53)?
14 Explain 'she is getting close to breaking point' (line 54).
15 What does Alison mean when she says 'Well, does it look like it!' (line 62)?

Practice unit 4.3

Read the text slowly and carefully, and then answer the questions that follow.

Helping black teenagers to read

There have been substantial numbers of black children in Britain's secondary schools for many years now, but most of the reading material available to them is still directed at the white majority. Carol Bergman, a young American who taught remedial reading classes for the Inner London Education Authority from 1968 until last year, believes that the lack of material to appeal directly to black students is part of the reason many of them 5 need remedial reading at secondary level.

She has therefore written three short books for Heinemann Educational Books, in which the heroes are black children in situations which will be familiar to many black pupils.

Practice unit 4.3

Although weak on plot in the conventional sense, the books are packed with incident. In one a schoolgirl runs away from home when she discovers she is pregnant. In another the hero, a teenager who cannot read, is suspended from school for pushing a teacher over.

Mrs Bergman thinks realism and honesty are important if the books are to fulfil their purpose. Thus there is a scene in one of them in which a black and a white boy, both in the same class, go to see the careers officer. The white boy is given a chit for a job interview, but when the black boy goes he is told the job market is bad. This is one of the factors contributing to his anger and his assault on the teacher.

'This happens,' Mrs Bergman told me. 'There is much higher unemployment among black school-leavers than white. It doesn't help to lie about the fact that there is discrimination and that it's harder for black kids.'

In the same way she thinks she has been honest about the schoolgirl's pregnancy. 'I make no moral statement about pregnancy', she said. 'I leave it deliberately open-ended. People are going to get pregnant no matter what you do.

'I hope it will stimulate discussion about what the girl should do. The important thing is that she goes back to her mother to discuss it and try to sort out what she should do. It will be resolved within the family.'

In the book about the violent boy – based on one of her former pupils – the headmaster is shown as sympathetic to him, trying to find the reason for his anger. Mrs Bergman, however, finds this comparatively rare among teachers in real life.

'The teachers do not try to find out what is troubling them. They treat the symptoms, not the causes. Children get angry and they don't know why, and sometimes this anger interferes with their ability to read.

'Teachers have come up to me very often and said: "How do I begin to talk to these kids?" That's very odd. They come to me, a white American, and ask how to talk to West Indians.'

She hopes the books will lead children on to reading more solid stuff from the school library. 'I don't think to have them reading about their immediate background is the be-all and end-all of the educational process. But you have to start somewhere, and you may as well start where they are.'

Mrs Bergman is now a part-time tutor with the Open University, working at home to look after her year-old child. She does not plan any further similar books.

'It was a freak that I did these', she said. 'I only did it because I became impatient at the lack of suitable materials. Now the time has come for publishers to approach black teachers to write this sort of book.'
(From a report in *The Times*.)

Exercise

1. Why did Carol Bergman write these books?
2. In two or three sentences, say what she thinks is important in preparing reading materials for black pupils.
3. Write more simply the expression 'substantial numbers of' (line 1).
4. What is meant by 'remedial reading' (line 6)?
5. The books are described as 'weak on plot in the conventional sense' (line 9). What do you think this means?
6. '...if the books are to fulfil their purpose' (lines 12–13). What is their purpose?
7. Rewrite in simpler language the expression 'one of the factors contributing to his anger' (lines 15–16).

Practice unit 4.3

8 'This happens' (line 17). What happens?
9 What does 'it' refer to in the expression 'it's harder for black kids' (line 19)?
10 What does Mrs Bergman mean by saying 'I leave it deliberately open-ended' (line 21)?
11 In the expression 'it will stimulate discussion' (line 23), what does 'it' refer to?
12 And what does 'it' mean in the expression 'to discuss it' (line 24)?
13 Who does 'his' refer to, in 'his anger' (line 27)?
14 'Mrs Bergman, however, finds this comparatively rare...' (lines 27–8). What is 'this'?
15 Who or what does 'them' refer to in the expression 'what is troubling them' (line 29)?
16 Why was it odd that teachers should ask Carol Bergman how to talk to black pupils?
17 What do you think is meant by 'more solid stuff from the school library' (lines 35–6)?
18 Rewrite in a different way the expression 'the be-all and end-all of the educational process' (lines 36–7).
19 Who does the word 'you' refer to, in the expression 'you have to start somewhere' (line 37)?
20 'You may as well start where they are' (lines 37–8). What does this mean?

Teaching unit 5: Writing summaries

Read this text slowly and carefully, and then go on to the instructions and exercise which which follow.

War

One day War and Kar were working on this garden (a jointly owned one) with their wives. War returned to the hamlet... He gave his own wife orders to weed a certain portion of the garden before he returned the next afternoon. When he returned he found the work not yet done. He asked his wife for an explanation, and she said that she had been possessed by a ghost the night before... Kar's wife said that this was not the explanation at all. The real reason why the work was undone, she said, was that the woman had spent the morning in the bushes with Kar. War became furious at this, knocked his wife down with his fist, and threatened to spear his brother Kar... War's wife returned in a fury to the hamlet, packed her things, took her young daughter by the hand and left before War returned... When War returned that evening and found his wife gone, he was even more angry than before... The next day he traced her to Yelagu, a neighboring tribe... He took three spears and set out alone to bring back his runaway wife. Someone warned the Yelagu that he was coming, so that when he arrived there was only a cripple left in the village. War demanded where his wife had gone, but the cripple either could not or would not tell him and offered him a dog and some shell money if War would spare his life. War demanded more money, took it and the dog, and returned home.

The next evening War called his friends together. He distributed the dog meat among them, told them what had happened, and suggested that they go on a head-hunting raid against the Yelagu. He argued that it was a very small tribe and that they were all cowards ... Most of those present thought that it was a good idea, but several objected on the grounds that Yelagu was too near Ambunti, the government post... They said that it would be much safer to attack Sowal, a tribe far in the swamp...

For two weeks there was a great deal of discussion... The other men of the tribe, meanwhile, had been swayed by the argument that there was considerable danger of punishment from the whites if Yelagu were attacked, whereas Sowal involved much less danger. It was also reported that high water had driven the Sowal out of their central village, and that they were living on knolls in small isolated groups that would be particularly vulnerable. The pressure of these arguments finally forced War to give up his idea of attacking Yelagu, and he threw his weight into planning for the Sowal raid...

War and some of the older men of the hamlet began to incite the young men to go on the raid. He told them that this was their chance to become big men...

Finally, all the men of the subtribe and some from neighbouring tribes met one night

Teaching unit 5

at the house tamberan near War's house...It was decided to send a scout ahead to discover the lay of the land...

The next day the scout returned to say that the road to Sowal was impassable. The water was so high that it was impossible to walk there, but it was not high enough to go with a canoe. The raid was therefore called off. I think that if it had not been for many who feared punishment from the whites, a way would have been found and the raid carried out.
(From *Becoming a Kwoma* by J. M. Whiting)

Suppose you had to answer the following question:

Sum up the main events described in the passage in a paragraph of not more than 100 words.

How would you go about it?
   This type of test (often called 'summary' or 'précis') is not difficult if you follow a system. One possible approach is to go through the following steps:
1. Read through the text from beginning to end, underlining all the points which should come into your answer. Do this very carefully, and be careful not to miss anything important.
2. Make a list of notes, in which you reproduce very briefly in your own words all the points you've underlined. It might look like this:
   – War's wife didn't do work in garden
   – she said because of ghost
   – Kar's wife said because of Kar
   – War very angry
   – wife ran away with daughter to Yeluga tribe
   – War went after her
   – didn't find her
   – asked friends to help him attack Yel.
   – friends said too near white men
   – preferred attack Sowal (far away, flood)
   – 2 weeks' discussion
   – decision attack S.
   – scout sent ahead
   – returned, said impossible reach Sowal
   This list contains all the essential points of the original text, but some of the less important details have been left out (for instance, War's threat to kill his brother, and the details of his visit to the Yelagu village). Note that a good list is long from top to bottom (it's got plenty of points in), but short from left to right (each point is expressed as briefly as possible).
3. Without looking at the original text, join these points together into a paragraph. Change the order of the points if necessary, to make the construction more logical. Use conjunctions, participle constructions, and adverbs like 'therefore' or 'however' to show the connections between ideas. Drop some more details if the paragraph looks like being too long.
4. Look back at the text and check that you have produced a good summary of what was said, in good English and in the right number of words. If you are not completely satisfied, make whatever improvements are necessary and rewrite the paragraph.
Here is a possible summary of the text about War:

'War and his wife quarrelled about her work and her relationship with War's brother, so she took their daughter and went to the Yelagu. War went after her, but could not find her; on his return, he asked his friends to help him attack the Yelagu. However, they felt that it would be safer to attack the Sowal, who lived further away from the white men and whose village was flooded. After two weeks' discussion, War agreed and they planned the attack. A scout was sent ahead, but when he returned he said it was impossible to reach Sowal.'

Exercise

In a paragraph of not more than sixty words, summarise what the passage tells us about War's aggressive behaviour.

Practice unit 5.1

Read the text slowly and carefully, and then answer the questions which follow.

Summerhill education and standard education

I hold that the aim of life is to find happiness, which means to find interest. Education should be a preparation for life. Our culture has not been very successful. Our education, politics, and economics lead to war. Our medicines have not done away with disease. Our religion has not abolished usury and robbery. Our boasted humanitarianism still allows public opinion to approve of the barbaric sport of hunting. The advances of the age are advances in mechanism – in radio and television, in electronics, in jet planes. New world wars threaten, for the world's social conscience is still primitive.

If we feel like questioning today, we can pose a few awkward questions. Why does man seem to have many more diseases than animals have? Why does man hate and kill in war when animals do not? Why does cancer increase? Why are there so many suicides? So many insane sex crimes? Why the hate that is anti-Semitism? Why Negro hating and lynching? Why back-biting and spite? Why is sex obscene and a leering joke? Why is being a bastard a social disgrace? Why the continuance of religions that have long ago lost their love and hope and charity? Why, a thousand whys about our vaunted state of civilized eminence!

I ask these questions because I am by profession a teacher, one who deals with the young. I ask these questions because those so often asked by teachers are the unimportant ones, the ones about school subjects. I ask what earthly good can come out of discussions about French or ancient history or what not when these subjects don't matter a jot compared to the larger question of life's natural fulfilment – of man's inner happiness.

How much of our education is real doing, real self-expression? Handwork is too often the making of a pin tray under the eye of an expert. Even the Montessori system, well-known as a system of directed play, is an artificial way of making the child learn by doing. It has nothing creative about it.

In the home, the child is always being taught. In almost every home, there is always at least one ungrown-up grownup who rushes to show Tommy how his new engine works. There is always someone to lift the baby up on a chair when baby wants to examine

Practice unit 5.1

something on the wall. Every time we show Tommy how his engine works we are stealing from that child the joy of life – the joy of discovery – the joy of overcoming an obstacle. Worse! We make that child come to believe that he is inferior, and must depend on help.

Parents are slow in realizing how unimportant the learning side of school is. Children, like adults, learn what they want to learn. All prize-giving and marks and exams sidetrack proper personality development. Only pedants claim that learning from books is education.

Books are the least important apparatus in a school. All that any child needs is the three R's;* the rest should be tools and clay and sports and theatre and paint and freedom.

Most of the school work that adolescents do is simply a waste of time, of energy, of patience. It robs youth of its right to play and play and play; it puts old heads on young shoulders.

When I lecture to students at teacher training colleges and universities, I am often shocked at the ungrownupness of these lads and lasses stuffed with useless knowledge. They know a lot; they shine in dialectics; they can quote the classics – but in their outlook on life many of them are infants. For they have been taught *to know*, but have not been allowed *to feel*. These students are friendly, pleasant, eager, but something is lacking – the emotional factor, the power to subordinate thinking to feeling. I talk to these of a world they have missed and go on missing. Their textbooks do not deal with human character, or with love, or with freedom, or with self-determination. And so the system goes on, aiming only at standards of book learning – goes on separating the head from the heart.

It is time that we were challenging the school's notion of work. It is taken for granted that every child should learn mathematics, history, geography, some science, a little art, and certainly literature. It is time we realized that the average young child is not much interested in any of these subjects.

I prove this with every new pupil. When told that the school is free, every new pupil cries, 'Hurrah! You won't catch me doing dull arithmetic and things!'

I am not decrying learning. But learning should come after play. And learning should not be deliberately seasoned with play to make it palatable.

Learning is important – but not to everyone. Nijinsky could not pass his school exams in St Petersburg, and he could not enter the State Ballet without passing those exams. He simply could not learn school subjects – his mind was elsewhere. They faked an exam for him, giving him the answers with the papers – so a biography says. What a loss to the world if Nijinsky had had really to pass those exams!

Creators learn what they want to learn in order to have the tools that their originality and genius demand. We do not know how much creation is killed in the classroom with its emphasis on learning.

I have seen a girl weep nightly over her geometry. Her mother wanted her to go to the university, but the girl's whole soul was artistic. I was delighted when I heard that she had failed her college entrance exams for the seventh time. Possibly, the mother would now allow her to go on the stage as she longed to do.

Some time ago, I met a girl of fourteen in Copenhagen who had spent three years in Summerhill and had spoken perfect English here. 'I suppose you are at the top of your class in English,' I said.

She grimaced ruefully. 'No, I'm at the bottom of my class, because I don't know English grammar,' she said. I think that disclosure is about the best commentary on what adults consider education.

Indifferent scholars who, under discipline, scrape through college or university and

---

* *the three R's*: reading, writing and arithmetic

Practice unit 5.1

become unimaginative teachers, mediocre doctors, and incompetent lawyers would possibly be good mechanics or excellent bricklayers or first-rate policemen.

We have found that the boy who cannot or will not learn to read until he is, say, fifteen is always a boy with a mechanical bent who later on becomes a good engineer or electrician. I should not dare dogmatize about girls who never go to lessons, especially to mathematics and physics. Often such girls spend much time with needlework, and some, later on in life, take up dressmaking and designing. It is an absurd curriculum that makes a prospective dressmaker study quadratic equations or Boyle's Law.

Caldwell Cook wrote a book called *The Play Way*, in which he told how he taught English by means of play. It was a fascinating book, full of good things, yet I think it was only a new way of bolstering the theory that learning is of the utmost importance. Cook held that learning was so important that the pill should be sugared with play. This notion that unless a child is learning something the child is wasting his time is nothing less than a curse – a curse that blinds thousands of teachers and most school inspectors. Fifty years ago the watchword was 'Learn through doing.' Today the watchword is 'Learn through playing.' Play is thus used only as a means to an end, but to what good end I do not really know.

(From *Summerhill* by A. S. Neill)

Exercise

1. What does Neill regard as the basis of happiness?
2. What does he feel about our culture?
3. Sum up what he says about the behaviour of civilised people.
4. What is meant by the word 'one', in line 16?
5. Why, according to Neill, are the questions so often asked by teachers unimportant (line 17)?
6. What does the word 'ones', in the expression 'the ones about school subjects' (lines 17–18) refer to?
7. Explain the meaning of 'a jot' (line 19).
8. In line 25, Neill says 'the child is always being taught'. Does he consider this a good or a bad thing?
9. Who is 'Tommy' (line 26)?
10. What is meant by saying that exams etc. 'sidetrack' proper personality development (lines 32–3)?
11. What is 'the rest' in line 35?
12. 'It robs youth of its right...' (line 37). What do 'it' and 'its' refer to?
13. Explain 'it puts old heads on young shoulders' (lines 37–8).
14. 'I talk to these of a world they have missed' (lines 44–5). Who are 'these'?
15. Explain what Neill means by 'separating the head from the heart' (line 47).
16. In the expression 'I prove this' (line 52), what does 'this' refer to?
17. Rewrite in another way 'learning should not be deliberately seasoned with play to make it palatable' (lines 54–5).
18. What is meant by the expression 'the pill should be sugared' (line 86)?
19. According to what is said in lines 86–8, does Neill feel that if a child is not learning something he is wasting his time?
20. In a paragraph of about 100 words, sum up Neill's views on education.

Practice unit 5.2

Read the text slowly and carefully, and then answer the questions that follow.

Hypnosis

There are many methods of producing hypnosis; indeed, almost every experienced hypnotist employs variations differing slightly from those of others. Perhaps the most common method is something along these lines. The hypnotist tries to obtain his subject's co-operation by pointing out to him the advantages to be secured by the hypnosis, such as, for instance, the help in curing a nervous illness to be derived from the patient's remembering in the trance certain events which otherwise are inaccessible to his memory. The patient is reassured about any possible dangers he might suspect to be present in hypnosis, and he may also be told (quite truthfully) that it is not a sign of instability or weakness to be capable of being put in a hypnotic trance, but that, quite on the contrary, a certain amount of intelligence and concentration on the part of the subject is absolutely essential.

    Next, the subject is asked to lie down on a couch, or sit in an easy-chair. External stimulation is reduced to a minimum by drawing the curtains and excluding, as far as possible, all disruptive noises. It is sometimes helpful to concentrate the subject's attention on some small bright object dangled just above eye-level, thus forcing him to look slightly upwards. This leads quickly to a fatigue of the eye-muscles, and thus facilitates his acceptance of the suggestion that he is feeling tired and that his eyes are closing. The hypnotist now begins to talk to the subject in a soft tone of voice, repeating endlessly suggestions to the effect that the subject is feeling drowsy, getting tired, that his eyes are closing, that he is falling into a deep sleep, that he cannot hear anything except the hypnotist's voice, and so on and so forth. In a susceptible subject, a light trance is thus induced after a few minutes, and the hypnotist now begins to deepen this trance and to test the reactions of the subject by giving suggestions which are more and more difficult of execution. Thus, he will ask the subject to clasp his hands together, and tell him that it is impossible for him to separate his hands again. The subject, try as he may, finds, to his astonishment, that he cannot in actual fact pull his hands apart. Successful suggestions of this kind are instrumental in deepening the hypnotic trance until, finally, in particularly good subjects, all the phenomena which will be discussed presently can be elicited.

    Having induced a reasonably deep hypnotic trance in our subject, what types of phenomena can be elicited? The first and most obvious one, which, indeed, may be responsible in large measure for all the others, is a tremendous increase in the subject's suggestibility. He will take up any suggestion the hypnotist puts forward and act on it to the best of his ability. Suggest to him that he is a dog, and he will go down on all fours and rush around the room barking and yelping. Suggest to him that he is Hitler, and he will throw his arms about and produce an impassioned harangue in an imitation of the raucous tones of the Führer! This tremendous increase in suggestibility is often exploited on the stage to induce people to do foolish and ridiculous acts. Such practices are not to be encouraged because they go counter to the ideal of human dignity and are not the kind of way in which hypnosis ought to be used; nevertheless, they must be mentioned because it is probably phenomena such as these which are most familiar to people from vaudeville acts, from reading the papers, and so forth.

    It would not be true to say, however, that all suggestions are accepted, even in the very deepest trance. This is particularly true when a suggestion is made which is contrary to the ethical and moral conceptions held by the subject. A well-known story may be quoted to illustrate this. Charcot, the great French neurologist, whose classes at one time were attended by Freud, was lecturing on hypnosis and was demonstrating the phenomena of the hypnotic trance on a young girl of eighteen. When she had been hypnotized deeply he was called away, and handed over the demonstration to one of his assistants. This young man, lacking the seriousness of purpose so desirable in students of medicine, even French ones, suggested to the young lady that she should remove her clothes. She immediately awakened from her trance, slapped his face, and flounced out of the room, very much to his discomfiture.

(Abridged; from *Sense and Nonsense in Psychology* by H. J. Eysenck)

Exercise

1 What does the word 'others', in line 2, refer to?
2 In the expression 'along these lines', in line 3, what does 'these' mean?
3 Who or what is 'his subject' (line 3)?
4 Say briefly in your own words how a hypnotist 'tries to obtain his subject's co-operation' (lines 3–4).
5 Rewrite more simply 'which...are inaccessible to his memory' (line 6).
6 Why does a hypnotist sometimes use a bright object?
7 What is meant by 'a susceptible subject' (line 21)?
8 What is meant by the expression 'more and more difficult of execution' (lines 23–4)?
9 What is 'it' in the expression 'act on it' (line 32)?
10 Rewrite in another way the expression 'to the best of his ability' (lines 32–3).
11 What does the expression 'such practices' (line 37) refer to?
12 What does the author feel about the use of hypnosis in entertainment (third paragraph)?
13 What is 'this' in the expression 'this is particularly true' (line 43)?
14 Write more simply 'a suggestion...which is contrary to the ethical and moral conceptions held by the subject' (lines 43–4).
15 What is the purpose of the story at the end of the passage?
16 Sum up the most important points of the passage in a paragraph of around 100 words.

Practice unit 5.3

Read the text slowly and carefully, and then answer the questions that follow.

The Alcatraz manifesto

(In November 1969, a group of American Indians took over Alcatraz Island, in San Francisco Bay. Their purpose was to draw world attention to the way Indians were treated by the U.S. authorities. Despite the government's efforts to make them give up (for instance, by cutting off electricity and water), they continued to occupy the island until they were removed by force a year and a half later.)

PROCLAMATION:
To the Great White Father and All His People
  We, the native Americans, re-claim the land known as Alcatraz Island in the name of all American Indians by right of discovery.
  We wish to be fair and honorable in our dealings with the Caucasian* inhabitants of this land, and hereby offer the following treaty:
  We will purchase said Alcatraz Island for twenty-four dollars (24) in glass beads and red cloth, a precedent set by the white man's purchase of a similar island about 300 years ago. We know that $24 in trade goods for these 16 acres is more than was paid when Manhattan Island was sold, but we know that land values have risen over the years.
  We will give to the inhabitants of this island a portion of the land for their own to be held in trust by the Bureau of Indian Affairs and by the Bureau of Caucasian Affairs to hold in perpetuity – for as long as the sun shall rise and the rivers go down to the sea. We will further guide the inhabitants in the proper way of living. We will offer them our religion, our education, our life-ways, in order to help them achieve our level of civilization and thus raise them and all their white brothers up from their savage and unhappy state. We offer this treaty in good faith and wish to be fair and honorable in our dealings with all white men.
  We feel that this so-called Alcatraz Island is more than suitable for an Indian reservation, as determined by the white man's own standards. By this we mean that this place resembles most Indian reservations in that:
  1. It is isolated from modern facilities, and without adequate means of transportation.
  2. It has no fresh running water.
  3. It has inadequate sanitation facilities.
  4. There are no oil or mineral rights.
  5. There is no industry and so unemployment is very great.
  6. There are no health care facilities.
  7. The soil is rocky and non-productive; and the land does not support game.
  8. There are no educational facilities.
  9. The population has always exceeded the land base.
  10. The population has always been held as prisoners and kept dependent upon others.
  Further, it would be fitting and symbolic that ships from all over the world, entering the Golden Gate, would first see Indian land, and thus be reminded of the true history of this nation. This tiny island would be a symbol of the great lands once ruled by free and noble Indians. What use will we make of this land? Since the San Francisco Indian Center burned down, there is no place for Indians to assemble and carry on tribal life here in the white man's city. Therefore, we plan to develop on this island several Indian institutions:
    1. A CENTER FOR NATIVE AMERICAN STUDIES
    2. AN AMERICAN INDIAN SPIRITUAL CENTER
    3. AN INDIAN CENTER OF ECOLOGY
    4. A GREAT INDIAN TRAINING SCHOOL
  Some of the present buildings will be taken over to develop an AMERICAN INDIAN MUSEUM which will depict our native food and other cultural contributions we have given to the world. Another part of the museum will present some of the things the white man has given to the Indians in return for the land and life he took: disease, alcohol, poverty and cultural decimation (as symbolized by old tin cans, barbed wire, rubber tires, plastic containers, etc.). Part of the museum will remain a dungeon to symbolize both those Indian captives who were incarcerated for challenging white authority, and those who

* *Caucasian*: of European origin

Practice unit 5.3

were imprisoned on reservations. The museum will show the noble and the tragic events of Indian history, including the broken treaties, the documentary of the Trail of Tears, the Massacre of Wounded Knee, as well as the victory over Yellow Hair Custer and his army. 50

    In the name of all Indians, therefore, we re-claim this island for our Indian nations, for all these reasons. We feel this claim is just and proper, and that this land should rightfully be granted to us for as long as the rivers shall run and the sun shall shine. 55

Signed,
Indians Of All Tribes
November 1969
San Francisco, California

(From *Protest USA*)

Exercise

1. Alcatraz was used for a particular purpose some time before the Indian occupation. Can you find any evidence in the passage to suggest what this purpose was?
2. What is meant by the expression 'the Great White Father and All His People' (line 2)?
3. Why do the Indians call themselves 'the native Americans' (line 3)?
4. Explain why the Indians use the expression 'by right of discovery' (line 4).
5. Why do they only offer 24 dollars' worth of goods for Alcatraz?
6. What exactly was 'a similar island' (line 8)?
7. What is the point of their offer of a special place for the white inhabitants of the island to live in (lines 11–13)?
8. Why do they say that they want to 'raise them and all their white brothers up from their savage and unhappy state' (lines 16–17)?
9. What is meant by the following expressions?
a) 'modern facilities' (line 22)
b) 'sanitation facilities' (line 24)
c) 'health care facilities' (line 27)
d) 'educational facilities' (line 29)
10. Explain simply 'The soil is rocky and non-productive; and the land does not support game' (line 28).
11. What is meant by 'the population has always exceeded the land base' (line 30)?
12. What is the attitude of the Indians to white American culture, as shown in the passage?
13. What are the American Indians' reasons for protest, as stated directly or indirectly in the passage? Answer in a paragraph of around 100 words.

Practice unit 5.4

Read the text slowly and carefully, and then answer the questions that follow.

The marriages that Britain splits up

Caroline Pond sets off on Thursday on a 4,500-mile journey to visit her husband, Daniel, and two step-children. Against their will, she and Daniel are forced to live in different continents.

The reason: Caroline is one of hundreds of British wives who are victims of a law which prevents their foreign husbands joining them in this country. This law makes it almost impossible for a British woman to marry a foreigner – unless she is prepared to live in her husband's native country. But the law, which was intended to reduce the number of immigrants coming into the United Kingdom, does not apply to the British male who marries a foreign woman. He is legally entitled to bring her to live with him in this country.

'In the eyes of the law, women are second-class citizens,' Caroline says. 'In this country, we have about as many rights as a dog which belongs to a man.'

Caroline, 27, is a demonstrator in physiology in the Zoology Department at Oxford University; Daniel is an associate professor of biology at Michigan University. Before they married eight months ago, she applied to the Home Office for permission for him to live in Britain. 'It is a waste of time,' she says. 'The answer is always "never".'

For the sake of her career, Caroline wishes to stay in her job for at least another 18 months and the couple were hoping to live in the small Victorian house she owns at Oxford. Ideally, while his wife is at the university, Daniel would have liked to come here and write scientific text-books.

'We have both accepted that I should be the breadwinner,' Caroline says. 'Daniel has always looked after the children and would continue to do so. I cannot understand why there is this discrimination against women. After all, I pay the same taxes as a man.'

However, they have now resigned themselves to a commuter marriage for the next 18 months. During their courtship and marriage, Daniel and Caroline have already crossed the Atlantic 20 times between them. 'We are lucky, because we can afford to pay the fares, but there must be many women who cannot,' she says.

Before she leaves finally to make her home in the United States, she is determined to campaign for the reform of the law. 'I feel very strongly that if it is the last thing I do before I have to live in America, it should be for this cause.'

The discriminatory measure, unchallenged in the House of Commons, was introduced in 1969 by James Callaghan, then Home Secretary. He described it as an 'administrative measure' to stop abuse of the law which allowed a male Commonwealth citizen to enter this country if he could prove that he was to marry a British girl.

Two years later under the Conservatives, the Immigration Act took the matter even further by stating that *no* foreign husband married to a British girl 'has claim to settlement in right of his wife unless...the (Home) Secretary is satisfied that there are special considerations, whether of a family nature or otherwise, which render exclusion undesirable'.

Mrs Mary Dines, of the Joint Council for the Welfare of Immigrants, says that hardship has now been defined by test cases as meaning that the wife would, if forced to live in her husband's country, suffer through political persecution, race, creed or difference of culture.

She comments: 'If you can prove you were marrying a Nigerian and would have to

Practice unit 5.4

live in the bush, you would probably get off; but if you were marrying someone from, say, Cyprus, Greece or America, you wouldn't stand a chance.' 45

Moves are now afoot in both Houses of Parliament to end this discrimination. In the Lords, the Labour peer Lord Brockway has tabled a motion on equal immigration rights for women; and Mrs Lynda Chalker, the new Conservative M.P. for Wallasey, will put down a question in the Commons this week.

Mrs Chalker is collecting a dossier of cases – already she has more than 150. She believes that few British women are fully aware of the problems they may encounter if they consider marrying a foreigner and feels that more publicity should be given to the possible consequences. 'We should let the poor girls know what they are letting themselves in for,' she says.

(Report by Wendy Hughes in *The Sunday Times*)

Exercise

1. What is the '4,500-mile journey' referred to in line 1?
2. According to the passage, is it illegal for Englishwomen to marry foreigners?
3. What is unfair about the law relating to immigration and marriage, as described in the text?
4. Who are 'we' in line 12?
5. Explain the expression 'for the sake of her career' (line 17).
6. What is the meaning of the word 'breadwinner' (line 21)?
7. What does the writer mean by a 'commuter marriage' (line 24)?
8. What is 'this cause' (line 30)?
9. In the expression 'he described it' (line 32), what is 'it'?
10. Rewrite the expression 'no foreign husband has claim to settlement in right of his wife' (lines 36–7) in simpler language.
11. State simply under what conditions a foreign husband would be allowed to settle in Britain, according to the passage.
12. What is meant by 'you would probably get off' (line 44)?
13. What is meant by 'you wouldn't stand a chance' (line 45)?
14. Explain the expression 'what they are letting themselves in for' (lines 53–4).
15. In a paragraph of around 100 words, explain the legal position of foreigners who married British people at the time when the article was written, and the effect that this had on Mr and Mrs Pond.

Practice unit 5.5

Read the text slowly and carefully, and then answer the questions that follow.

Nightmare in a California jail

When I moved my family to San Francisco last year to teach in the English department at San Francisco State College, I did so with misgivings. I knew that the educational atmosphere in California was far from tranquil – Governor Reagan was waging virtual war against student protesters, and the political polarization between the left and the right could only be described in terms of paranoia. Through the year, my fears were confirmed as I witnessed student and faculty strikes, bombings, brawls, police assaults, mass arrests. But none of those events – brutal as they were – prepared me for the nightmare that followed my recent chance arrest this spring in Berkeley. Overnight that experience, which can be verified by many reliable witnesses, turned a father of five, veteran of the Korean war, and law-abiding citizen into a bitter man.

On Thursday morning, 22 May, I left San Francisco State College with four other teachers to drive to Berkeley.

We arrived in Berkeley about noon. After a pleasant lunch and a trip to buy supplies we walked toward Shattuck on Addison Street. There we were to meet my friend's wife, Nora.

The city of Berkeley was then in something like a state of siege because of the People's Park issue. On the streets, under the command of Alameda County Sheriff Frank Madigan, was a vast force of National Guard troops, county sheriffs, San Francisco Tactical Squad units. Madigan had authorized use of shotguns against demonstrators. One man had already been killed, and many others wounded. Demonstrators, workers, and onlookers trapped in a plaza on the University of California campus had been sprayed from a helicopter with a virulent form of tear gas currently being used in Vietnam. To protest, approximately 2,000 students had now begun a spontaneous march from the University campus through downtown Berkeley.

We could see a concentration of National Guard troops, policemen and citizens several blocks east of us. I described what Nora looked like to the others and we stopped at the southwest corner of Shattuck and Addison to scan the crowd for her. We decided not to go any farther because we saw soldiers, police, and people both to the east and south of us.

Berkeley policemen and Alameda County deputies began moving our way. An officer leading four or five others approached our group of twelve to fifteen people and said, 'Let's move out; clear the area!' Everyone on our corner obediently started walking away. Suddenly, a Berkeley policeman ran in front of us, spread his arms and shouted, 'Stay where you are!' Behind us, two other policeman kept repeating, 'Keep moving, clear out of here!' We said we were leaving, and at this point a Berkeley police sergeant approached and began pointing to various people in our group, saying, 'Get that one, that one, that one.'

An officer snapped handcuffs on me and joined me with the cuffs to a protesting youngster. I asked if we were under arrest and the officer said yes – we were charged with blocking traffic. We were not allowed to talk to the policemen after that. The sergeant who had us arrested taunted us, using obscenities and accusing us of being revolutionaries, rock-throwers, and hippies. Those not fingered by the sergeant continued down the street and were not apprehended. While we were being herded into the paddy wagon,

Practice unit 5.5

however, officers continued to arrest people at random – mostly young people and particularly those with long hair, moustaches, sideburns. Three of the teachers with me were arrested; our fifth companion was not, and he immediately began calling friends and relatives to arrange our release.

Nineteen of us – seventeen men and two women – were packed into a paddy wagon. I was never able to identify myself or state my business; indeed, the policemen threatened anyone who talked at all. We sat in the wagon for about 20 minutes, then it backed up the street a block, where we were transferred to a large bus. We were all being taken to 'Santa Rita', a place I had never heard of.

During the 45-minute ride our feelings were reinforced that it had been an indiscriminate bust. Aboard were students with books and notepads who had been on their way to and from classes at the University. There was a US mailman (with long hair), still carrying his bag of mail, and a resident psychiatrist who had stepped outside his hospital for a short walk during a 30-minute break. Others included several young divinity students and five medical observers – young men in white smocks with red crosses – who had accompanied the student march down Shattuck Avenue. The police blew it, I thought. They went too far this time. Most of us will be released when we get to wherever we're going.

The bus stopped inside the Santa Rita Rehabilitation Center and Prison Farm, an institution run by Alameda County. We were marched into the compound and ordered to lie prone in rows. Those who looked around or stumbled or didn't move fast enough were prodded and hit with clubs. Frequently, men were dragged out of the marching lines and forced to kneel while being struck. The guards shouted and screamed, often giving conflicting commands and clubbing those unable to obey them. Our chief source of terror was not so much the beatings as the wild hysteria that had seized many of the guards. They walked up and down our rows of flattened men, striking upraised hands with clubs, striking us on the soles of our feet with clubs to make us lie in even rows. We were told we would be shot if we tried to escape. We were cursed continuously; we were called dope users, revolutionaries, filthy long-hairs. We would, they shouted, be taught such a lesson that we would never again cause trouble. All of us were identified as political troublemakers. No attempt was made to distinguish us by age, nature of charges, or physical condition. Periodically we were ordered to turn our heads to the left or right. I experienced severe leg cramps and sharp twinges of pain from an arthritic elbow. From time to time we were forced to close up ranks by crawling across the asphalt, which was covered with sharp gravel. Those accused of speaking or looking around or moving slightly were dragged out and forced to kneel with their hands behind them in a separate group. Some remained kneeling for hours. There were some 300 men on the ground.

The first thing I learned facedown on the Santa Rita asphalt was that I could make it without begging or breaking. This felt good; it was enough strength to counter the fears engendered by the heavy blue-black guards' shoes slowly crunching by my eyes six inches away. *But to be put to these tests in America!*
(Abridged; from *Getting Busted* by Jesse P. Ritter, Jr)

Exercise

1 Why was the author worried about going to work at San Francisco State College?
2 Explain the meaning of the expression 'My fears were confirmed' (line 5).
3 What was the reason for the protest march referred to in lines 22–4?
4 Why did the author describe Nora to the others?
5 What did the officer mean by the words 'Let's move out; clear the area!' (line 32)?

Practice unit 5.5

6 Why was it difficult for the author and his friends to obey the instructions of the police (lines 30–7)?
7 What does the expression 'fingered by the sergeant' (line 42) mean?
8 Comment on the reasons given in the passage for the writer's arrest.
9 On what basis were people chosen for arrest, according to the passage?
10 What did the writer learn during his 45-minute ride to Santa Rita?
11 What did the people who were arrested find most frightening in Santa Rita?
12 Describe, in two or three sentences, the attitude of the guards in Santa Rita.
13 What does the writer mean by 'I could make it' (the last paragraph)?
14 In a paragraph of around 120 words, sum up the writer's experiences.

Section C:
Practice tests

Practice test 1

Read the text slowly and carefully, and then answer the questions that follow.

Factory life – a student's experience

This summer, like many students, I took a job in a small factory to help subsidise my University grant during the coming term. Having just left school, I had never had a full-time job before and so I was quite looking forward to it. I decided to work for 8 weeks and thought it might even prove to be quite enjoyable. Here I made my biggest mistake ever! 5

   I dutifully turned up one cold morning in July at 8 a.m. all ready to start work. The factory produces bleach* and washing-up liquid. My first job was to feed empty plastic bottles onto the assembly line. The conveyor belt was divided into compartments and one bottle had to go in each compartment.

   As the belt was moving very fast, I could hardly keep up with it, and, spilling bottles 10
in all directions, I shouted over the din to the supervisor, 'What happens when you miss one?' Back came the grim reply 'You never miss one!' Oh well, only another $7\frac{1}{2}$ hours...

   The next day I was moved into the bleach department where I made up cardboard boxes and helped to fill them with full bottles of bleach. I found the sharp cardboard often cut into my hands and wrists and that the cuts were soon filled with bleach which splashed 15
over the bottles. Ironically the bottles themselves carried the warning: 'If splashed onto clothing or skin, wash immediately'! Of course the assembly line didn't stop when I wanted to wash the bleach from my cuts!

   Eventually I was given a pair of gloves, but these were only cotton and were in shreds by the end of the day. Also the plastic apron I had been given provided no protection for 20
my clothes.

   I walked home on the 2nd day, coughing because of the bleach fumes, my ears still ringing from the noise and my hands stinging. My enthusiasm was definitely wavering.

   During this first week, other 'exciting' jobs I was given included taking hot bottles from a printing machine (no gloves provided) and taking heavy boxes full of bottles from one end of the factory to the other. By the end of the week I was exhausted and bruised 26
and received for my troubles just over £17 (this was without paying tax).

   Talking to the regular workers, I found that they considered my week quite a nice one as I had at least had some variety. Many of them had done the same boring job year after year. One girl had been there for 9 years and her only job 8 hours a day was to put tops on bottles as they came past her on a conveyor belt. She couldn't even sit down. I was told

---

* *bleach*: a strong chemical used for cleaning

that she was mentally retarded. Whether this was the case before she started her job is another question!

In my second week I was put in the department where the bottles were made. Here the machines were liable to jam up and some even caught fire. When my machine jammed up I was casually told to put my hand in and pull out the hot plastic!

Many new parts were needed for the machines but the mechanics told me that a lot of the machines were German and some were very old, so that it was either too expensive or impossible to get new parts.

Meanwhile the machines constantly broke down or went wrong so that the workers spent most of their time endangering themselves by trying to work with them. During the short time that I have been there, there has been one broken leg, an injured arm and many burns.

As a lot of production is lost through the inefficiency of these machines the management make up for this by increasing the speed of the machines and the assembly lines until it is very difficult for the workers to keep up with them. Also in this department, there were two other mentally retarded people: one young girl who could not keep up with her machine at all, and one old bloke who often got caught up in wires and things whilst trying to clean the machines.

As the temperatures rose during the summer, the ventilation proved totally inadequate and we were working in temperatures well over 90 degrees. As if this was not bad enough, one day a leak developed in the main bleach container and the fumes were just overwhelming. For the first time in the history of the factory, the workers downed tools!

The management was amazed and quite unable to cope with the situation. Perhaps they thought their sleepy town was immune from such 'nonsense' – they were in for a surprise! Unfortunately a large number of workers (nearly all of them women, and a lot of them part-timers) were not members of the union and without this strength behind them, the workers were soon persuaded to return to work. But these workers learnt a lot from that very short strike and I feel sure that many of them will now join the union.

Now I am finishing work this week and I feel that in 8 weeks in the factory I have learnt much more about the nature of our society than I ever did in 7 years in a grammar school. A lot of what I saw and experienced I should like to forget, but that is not possible as during my 5th week I managed to sit on some boiling hot plastic which had spilled from the machine. So now I can never forget the factory – I am branded for life!
(Article by Jenny Smith in *Militant*)

Choose the correct answer to each question.

1   The writer took a job in a factory
a) to help subsidise her university.
b) to pay for her studies during the following term.
c) to add to the money she would have to pay for her studies.
d) to earn money for her summer holiday.

2   Her first job was
a) to empty plastic bottles on to the assembly line.
b) to produce bleach and washing-up liquid.
c) to feed bleach and washing-up liquid into plastic bottles.
d) to put bottles into compartments on the assembly belt.

Practice test 1

3 The worst feature of her second job was
a) a dangerous chemical splashing on her skin and clothes.
b) the bad cuts she got.
c) the speed of the assembly line.
d) the fact that she was working in the bleach department.

4 The writer's first week's experience of work was
a) quite nice.
b) exciting.
c) tiring and hard.
d) very dangerous.

5 She suggests that her first week's pay
a) all went in tax.
b) was not very much for the work she did.
c) was excellent.
d) was good enough for the job she did.

6 Many of the other workers
a) had mental trouble.
b) had worse jobs than the writer.
c) spent all their time putting tops on bottles.
d) had better jobs than the writer.

7 During her second week the writer
a) found her work dangerous.
b) enjoyed herself more than she had the week before.
c) spent her time repairing machines.
d) spent her time filling plastic bottles with jam.

8 In the expression 'make up for this' (line 45), the word 'this' refers to
a) the speed of the machines.
b) the machines.
c) the inefficiency of the machines.
d) the lost production.

9 What was the cause of the machine's inefficiency?
a) The workers couldn't keep up with them.
b) The plastic got hot.
c) Spare parts were difficult to get.
d) They kept jamming.

10 What does 'this' refer to, in the expression 'As if this was not bad enough' (line 51)?
a) the heat.
b) the ventilation.
c) the leak that developed.
d) the work.

Practice test 2

11 Why did the workers 'down tools' (line 53)?
a) to give the management a surprise
b) because of the heat and the gases that came from the bleach
c) Because they had no union.
d) Because the machines were dangerous.

12 Why did the workers soon return to work, according to the passage?
a) Because they had no union to support their protest.
b) Because the town had no tradition of strikes.
c) Because the management offered better conditions.
d) Because a lot of them were women.

13 The writer feels the value of the strike was
a) that it got better conditions for the workers.
b) that it gave the management a shock.
c) that it increased the strength of the workers.
d) that it was likely to make the workers more aware of the need to organise themselves.

14 The writer seems to feel that her experience in the factory
a) will soon be forgotten.
b) helped her to learn about trade unions.
c) was unpleasant but taught her a lot.
d) endangered her life.

Practice test 2

Read the text slowly and carefully, and then answer the questions that follow.

Who's crazy?

A bizarre experiment in the United States has demonstrated that psychiatrists cannot distinguish effectively between people who are mentally disturbed and those who are sane.

According to its originators, the experiment demonstrates the fallibility of conventional psychiatric diagnosis. It also lends considerable support to the position taken by radical psychiatrists like R. D. Laing, who argue that diagnoses of mental disease are often no more than convenient labels designed to make life easier for doctors.

Eight perfectly normal people, by shamming symptoms of a mild kind, successfully gained admission to psychiatric wards where they remained undetected for as long as they could stand it. Once admitted, their behaviour was normal in every way, but doctors and nurses continued to treat them as disturbed.

In every case but one the diagnosis was schizophrenia. Once they were labelled as mentally ill, everything the 'pseudopatients' did tended to confirm the diagnosis in the eyes of the medical staff, though other patients in the hospital were much less easy to convince.

The eight pseudopatients included three psychologists, a pediatrician, a psychiatrist, a

painter and a housewife. All eight assumed false names and those connected with the
medical profession also invented false occupations, so as not to attract special attention
from fellow-professionals. The hospitals chosen ranged from expensive private units to
dingy publicly-run institutions.

To gain admission the pseudo-patients told the whole truth about their lives, their
emotions and their personal relationships – all of which were within the normal range –
and lied only about their names, symptoms, and in some cases their occupations. The
symptoms they complained of were hearing disembodied voices saying the words 'empty',
'hollow' and 'thud'.

This was sufficient in every case for them to be classified as mentally ill. Once inside
they stopped pretending and behaved as normally as they could. Their stays inside varied
from 7 to 52 days, with an average of 19 days.

As many as a third of the real patients inside detected that they were frauds. 'You're not
crazy. You're a journalist or a professor. You're checking up on the hospital,' was a
typical comment from a fellow-patient.

The pseudopatients spent much of their time taking extensive notes, but even this did
not apparently raise any suspicions in the doctors' minds. 'Patient engages in writing
behaviour,' was the daily nursing comment on one patient, but nobody troubled to ask
him what he was writing.

The experiment was carried out under the supervision of Professor D. L. Rosenhan of
Stanford University, himself one of the eight fake patients. Writing about the experiment
in this week's *Science*, he concludes: 'We cannot distinguish the sane from the insane in
mental hospitals...how many people, one wonders, are sane but not recognised as such
in our psychiatric institutions?...How many have been stigmatised by well-intentioned,
but nevertheless erroneous, diagnoses?'

In Professor Rosenhan's view, the hospital itself is an environment that distorts judgment. As evidence, he quotes what happened to patients who asked doctors perfectly
sensible questions. They took the form: 'Pardon me, Dr X, could you tell me when I will
be eligible for ground privileges?' – or some similar request, courteously presented. In
almost threequarters of the cases the psychiatrist's response was to walk on, head averted.
Only one doctor in 25 stopped and tried to answer the question.

But the clinching piece of evidence comes from another experiment in which a hospital
was warned that pseudopatients would be presenting themselves. Faced with this threat
to their professional reputation, the doctors admitting patients became much more
conservative in their diagnosis. Of 193 patients presenting themselves, one doctor was
firmly convinced that 41 were frauds, while another doctor suspected 23. In fact, no fake
patients had arrived at all.

In the present state of knowledge, there seems little hope of more accurate diagnostics.
Doctors should try to err on the side of caution, in Rosenhan's opinion, and 'refrain from
sending the distressed to insane places'. That, and a more benign environment inside
institutions, could help to sort out the insane from the merely confused.
(Report by Nigel Hawkes in *The Observer*)

Choose the correct answer to each question.

1 The expression 'lends considerable support to', in line 5, means
a) helps for a short time
b) proves conclusively

Practice test 2

    c) helps to prove
    d) disproves

2 According to the passage, psychiatrists like R. D. Laing think
    a) that nobody is really mad.
    b) that doctors say patients are mentally ill in order to make things more convenient for the patients.
    c) that diagnoses of mental illness are not just convenient labels.
    d) that when somebody is diagnosed as having a 'mental illness', this often gives no real information about what is wrong with him.

3 The word 'who', in line 6, refers to
    a) R. D. Laing.
    b) doctors.
    c) psychiatrists.
    d) psychiatrists like Laing.

4 What does 'shamming' mean, in line 8?
    a) pretending to have
    b) having
    c) catching
    d) discussing

5 In the expression 'could stand it' (line 10), what does 'it' refer to?
    a) the pretence
    b) the strain and unpleasantness of the situation
    c) the physical conditions of the hospitals
    d) admission

6 The expression 'continued to treat them as disturbed' (line 11) means
    a) went on behaving towards them as if they were mentally ill
    b) treated them in a strange way the whole time
    c) consistently had an unusual attitude to them
    d) gave them a difficult time

7 According to the fourth paragraph of the report
    a) their mad behaviour in hospital fooled the doctors.
    b) the doctors and nurses regarded everything they did as mad.
    c) they made a great effort to imitate the behaviour of real mental patients.
    d) schizophrenics and normal people behave in the same way.

8 Why did some of the experimenters give false occupations?
    a) Because this is a symptom of schizophrenia.
    b) Because they wanted to hide their true personalities.
    c) They were doctors themselves, and they didn't want to be treated differently from normal patients.
    d) Because they didn't want to make the other patients suspicious.

Practice test 2

9 What is meant by 'pseudopatients' (line 16)?
a) a special category of patients
b) real patients
c) mental patients
d) people pretending to be patients

10 How did the experimenters manage to get admitted to mental hospitals?
a) by telling the whole truth about their emotional problems
b) by telling lies about their occupations and names
c) by saying that they heard voices saying words
d) by imitating schizophrenic behaviour

11 In the expression 'they were frauds' (line 29), who does 'they' refer to?
a) the experimenters
b) the real patients
c) a third of the real patients
d) the medical staff

12 What happened when the experimenters took notes?
a) The hospital staff didn't notice.
b) The hospital staff wanted to know what they were writing.
c) The hospital staff were suspicious.
d) The hospital staff seemed uninterested, or thought that the note-taking was a symptom of mental illness.

13 In the expression 'We cannot distinguish' (line 38), who does 'we' refer to?
a) the experimenters
b) psychiatrists
c) the public in general
d) mental patients

14 Why did the experimenters ask the doctors 'perfectly sensible questions' (lines 43–4)?
a) to prove that they were not mad
b) to see what the doctors would do
c) to ask for information
d) because they were bored

15 How did the doctors react to their questions?
a) 25 doctors answered them.
b) Three-quarters of the doctors got angry.
c) The majority treated the patients as if they didn't exist.
d) A quarter answered their questions.

16 When the experimenters asked the doctors questions
a) the experimenters behaved normally; the doctors behaved strangely.
b) the experimenters behaved strangely and the doctors behaved normally.
c) everybody behaved strangely.
d) everybody behaved normally.

17 Choose the best explanation of the expression 'faced with this threat to their professional reputation' (lines 49–50).
a) when they realised that they might lose their jobs
b) when they realised that they had made a lot of mistakes
c) in spite of the experimenters' theories
d) when they realised that their inability to distinguish between sane and mad people might be exposed

18 What happened in the second experiment, according to the report?
a) The doctors thought that a lot of genuine patients were pretending.
b) The doctors became less sure of themselves.
c) The doctors behaved in the opposite way from before.
d) The doctors found all the pseudopatients.

19 The two experiments seem to prove
a) that there is no difference between 'sane' and 'mad' people.
b) that many sane people are perhaps sent to mental hospitals.
c) that diagnosis of mental illness is impossible.
d) that most psychiatrists are not properly qualified.

Practice test 3

Read the text slowly and carefully, and then answer the questions that follow.

Control units

The controversial 'control unit' at Wakefield Prison is in use again. Three prisoners have been in the special punishment block since May 22, even though the Home Office hinted strongly three months ago that these deprivation cells were to be closed for good.

Sources within the Home Office suggested yesterday that the decision to reopen the cells had only been taken after long and often bitter official discussion. The reopening is seen as a victory for the hard-line position of the prison officers, and a corresponding defeat for those Home Office officials who felt that the control units caused more embarrassment to the prisons than effective discipline for their inmates.

The Home Secretary, Mr Jenkins, has shown his distaste for the control units but he is bound to consider the views of prison officers, who have been suggesting that without such special disciplinary procedures, authority within the prisons would be much harder to maintain. They have pointed to the recent controversy about the leniency of Mr Frank Leisching, governor of Winchester Prison, and the hundred warders (out of 180) who signed a motion of no confidence in his 'soft' approach.

Mr Jenkins told the Commons in February – after the situation had been exclusively revealed in *The Guardian* – that no prisoners were being considered for transfer to the then-empty control units. The second such unit at Wormwood Scrubs has now been dismantled.

Although Mr Jenkins suggested to Parliament that it was possible the units could be

Practice test 3

reopened should the disciplinary need arise, his statement was widely interpreted as a retreat from an unfortunate experiment by the Home Office.

The control units were introduced last year for inmates considered by prison staff to be 'intractable troublemakers'. Confinement in such a unit is divided into two stages. For the first 90 days the prisoner suffers solitary confinement for 23 hours of the day, relieved only by an hour of exercise in which he is forbidden to speak to other prisoners. Warders are trained to observe the prisoner without speaking to him except when absolutely necessary.

In the second stage, after the prisoner has gone through his first 90-day period without infringing the least rule, he is permitted to mix for a strictly-controlled part of the day with other inmates of the control cells. But if a single rule is breached – if a prisoner speaks to another inmate when he should not, or if he shows the slightest recalcitrance to a warder – he goes back to day one of the original regime.

These conditions, which have been criticised as brutal and medieval by prison reform groups and by several M.P.s and prisoners' relatives, were imposed on these latest three inmates after the recent disturbances in Hull.

Although the names of the three men serving these special terms are not known it is believed that at least two of them came originally from Hull prison.

Much of the new surge of prison discontent can be traced to the increasing tendency of courts to sentence criminals to long, and often to life, sentences. This, according to reform groups, has directly caused a new militancy among long-sentence prisoners, who feel they have little to lose.

Miss Gail Coles, of the Radical Alternatives to Prison group, said yesterday: 'The restoration of this vicious kind of punishment, in spite of every indication that this appalling experiment with human beings was to be abandoned, is a disgusting blot on the record of this Home Office.'
(Report by Martin Walker in *The Guardian*)

Choose the correct answer to each question.

1 A control unit is
a) a special kind of prison.
b) a part of a prison reserved for a special kind of punishment.
c) a particular kind of cell in a prison.
d) an experimental rehabilitation institute.

2 Why were the three men put in the control unit at Wakefield prison?
a) Because they caused disturbances at Hull prison.
b) Because they beat up a prison guard.
c) Because they spoke to other prisoners.
d) The article does not say clearly.

3 What do you think is meant by 'deprivation cells' (line 3)?
a) private rooms
b) places where the prisoners get no food or drink
c) places where the prisoners are isolated from human contact and the outside world
d) cells for bad prisoners

Practice test 3

4 What is meant by the expression 'hard-line position' (line 6)?
a) the view that it is difficult to control prisoners
b) a tough attitude towards prison discipline
c) a tendency towards self-pity
d) unwillingness to change

5 How can the attitudes of the Home Office and of the prison officers be compared, according to the article?
a) Most prison officers seem to have a tougher attitude than some Home Office officials.
b) They are in almost total agreement.
c) They are in almost total disagreement.
d) The article does not make the relative positions clear.

6 According to the article, some Home Office officials feel
a) that control units are too cruel.
b) that prison officers aren't doing their jobs properly.
c) that control units are a mistake and don't achieve their purpose.
d) that control units should be kept.

7 What is 'a motion of no confidence' (line 14)?
a) a kind of demonstration
b) a kind of strike
c) a kind of meeting
d) a kind of statement

8 Mr Leishing was criticised by the staff of his prison
a) for incompetence.
b) for his treatment of the prison officers.
c) for using the control units.
d) for his attitude to discipline and punishment.

9 According to the article, Mr Jenkins said in Parliament
a) that control units were not at that time in use.
b) that control units were to be closed down.
c) that control units were important.
d) that control units were an unfortunate experiment.

10 The expression 'should the need arise' (line 20) means
a) the need ought to arise
b) if the need arose
c) the need would probably arise
d) the need might arise

11 What does 'an unfortunate experiment by the Home Office' (line 21) refer to?
a) Home Office interference in the running of prisons
b) the disagreement with the prison officers
c) the closing of the control units
d) the setting up of control units

Practice test 3

12 Prisoners are put in control units for
a) violence towards other prisoners.
b) violence towards prison officers.
c) refusing to submit to prison discipline.
d) talking to other prisoners without permission.

13 Prisoners stay in control units for
a) a minimum of 180 days.
b) a maximum of 180 days.
c) 90 days or more.
d) two periods of up to 90 days.

14 What is meant by 'he goes back to day one of the original regime' (line 32)?
a) He starts the 180 days' punishment again.
b) He leaves the control unit.
c) He goes back to one of the cells he was in before.
d) He starts his prison sentence again.

15 What is meant by the expression 'they have little to lose' (line 41)?
a) Good behaviour won't bring their freedom much nearer.
b) They are badly treated.
c) They are very poor.
d) They have reasons for complaining against society.

16 What does the word 'this' refer to, in line 39?
a) the new surge
b) prison discontent
c) the length of sentences
d) the tendency of courts to give long sentences

17 The group 'Radical Alternatives to Prison' seem to be
a) in favour of control units.
b) violently opposed to control units.
c) not entirely in favour of control units.
d) neutral.

18 What attitude does the author of the article seem to have?
a) He is in favour of control units.
b) He is against control units.
c) He points out their advantages and disadvantages in an objective fashion.
d) He reports the facts and other people's views, but does not show his own opinion directly.

Practice test 4

Read the text slowly and carefully, and then answer the questions that follow.

American finds real world in Africa

'The real world', Willie Russell said, 'is out there in the village where you're needed. You got a reason to get up in the morning.' He gestured toward the Sahel, the fringe of the Sahara, where for the last two years, as a Peace Corps volunteer, he has hunted water for the still suffering survivors of West Africa's seven-year drought.

'It's the people and the world they make for themselves,' Russell, 26, an American black from Newan, Ga., said, sitting on a hotel terrace in Niger's pleasant, riverfront capital, but letting his thoughts drift to a mud and straw village 70 miles north in the parched savannas. 'The way they laugh at trouble and help each other out. Even in the worst days, I'd fall asleep at night listening to the big calibash drums beating for a holiday or a baptism.'

He spoke of simple pleasures: 'The expression on the people's faces when you hit water, 150 feet down, and they pass around that first sip. The food, man – it takes some getting used to, but there isn't anything like it in the States. And Sunday nights after the big market when the people all get together to sing and dance and visit all around, and maybe there's a wrestling match between two villages...

'Not too many big things, but I love it. These people taught me a hell of a lot about living.'

Russell had come to town, 6 miles over dirt roads, to pick up a load of cement for casing a new well and to talk with a reporter about what an American black finds in Africa.

'I was scared when I got here,' Russell said. 'Of the people, not the animals. Hell, I've only seen two snakes since I've been here. They went one way and I went the other. But quick. And the only crocodile I ever saw is in the museum here.

'I was afraid I couldn't relate to the people. There are times I think I could spend the rest of my life here, but I know, no matter how long I stay, I'll always be an American. No changing that.

'The frogs are always first to make the scene when you hit a well,' he laughed. 'Don't know how they get the word. Then the village chief shows up with a couple of scrawny necked chickens and maybe a bottle of palm wine.'

Russell learned Djerma, a tribal language in central Niger, in a few months: 'It's easy. The verbs never change.' Now he often goes for days without speaking a word of English.

'People passing through the village,' he said, 'often take me for a Ghanaian, because of my facial structure, I guess. They immediately start talking in the Hausa language. They don't much take me for a *borio bi* – an Afro-American.'

He doesn't wear the ba-boo, the long flowing African tunic, but he likes native-style embroidered shirts with wide, draw-string collars. 'Cool for this weather and easy to find in the market.'

Russell's house in Oulam, the village where he is now showing the people how to find water, doesn't have electricity, so he goes to bed early, around 9, and reads magazines from the United States by lantern light. Most days, he's up at 6, 'with the giraffes and hippos', trying to get as much of the hole dug as the climbing sun and rising humidity will allow. The projects he directs are all self-help, so everyone from the chief on down lends a hand.

What Russell likes most about Africa is the respect and affection shown for old people. 'My grandparents taught me to respect my elders. Grandpa was a sharecropper back in Georgia, and that's how he brought me up. Love, he always said, was a lifetime deal, not the garbage you see in the movies.'

What Russell misses most are Sunday mornings back home, church services and hymn singing in a clapboard Methodist church.

'These people here', he pointed toward the mosque, 'got their religion and I got mine. When I'm riding in a bush taxi, with the chickens and the goats and all those children, I just sit tight and everyone piles out to pray.'

He wants to bring his mother, Edna Russell, to Africa for a visit. Maybe even to stay.

'I think a lot about it, and all the good things she's done for me in her life,' he said. 'Mom does domestic work in Lookout Mountain, Tenn., working in other people's homes. She'd love it here. It would be a big cultural shock at first, like it was for me, but when she saw the work I'm doing, and the love I have for the people, I just know they're going to love her, too.

'I wrote her how the whole village stayed up all night to listen to the Ali–Foreman fight. Seven thousand people gathered around one radio in the marketplace. I tell her to come out and join the real world.'

Mrs Russell just sends him a can of his favorite pipe tobacco and tells him to come home to the United States. 'Maybe I will,' Russell mused. 'But she ought to come see it before it's too late.'

Russell knows that the Africa he loves already has begun to vanish. The oil boom in neighbouring Nigeria is bringing electrical power to the bush villages and replacing the camels and donkeys with trucks and motorbikes. The twilight glow of the cooking fires, scenting the woodlands with West Africa's spicy herbal perfumes, is fading fast in the advance of the kerosene stove.

'How can I weep for an underdeveloped country that's starting to develop? That's why I came here, isn't it?'

(Report by Hugh A. Mulligan in *International Herald Tribune*)

1 'You got a reason to get up in the morning' (lines 1–2). What reason do you think he has in mind?
a) There is important work to do.
b) You have to get up early because everyone else does.
c) The place is so interesting that you want to see as much as possible.
d) It's too hot to stay in bed.

2 What is Willie Russell's job?
a) helping the inhabitants of a mud and straw village to modernise their way of life
b) working with a group that wants to change the Africans' way of life
c) going from one village to another showing the people how to find water and build wells
d) taking water to people who are suffering from the drought

3 What is meant by 'even in the worst days' (lines 8–9)?
a) even when he was most depressed
b) even when there was very little rain
c) even when he was exhausted by his work
d) even when the people were suffering most from lack of water

4 What did Willie Russell mean by 'there isn't anything like it in the States' (line 13)?
a) It's a new experience.
b) It's quite different from American food.
c) It's not so good as American food.
d) It's better than American food.

5 What was he most afraid of when he went to Africa?
a) snakebite
b) being attacked by the people
c) not being able to get on with the people
d) being prevented by the language barrier from communicating with them

6 What does the expression 'make the scene' mean, in line 27?
a) make a noise
b) arrive
c) spread themselves around the landscape
d) jump into the well

7 What does William Russell look like, to the local people?
a) an African from a different country
b) one of themselves
c) an American negro
d) a West Indian negro

8 Why does he get up early?
a) to be able to see the giraffes and hippos
b) because there is a lot of work to be done
c) because it's light at 6 o'clock
d) to get enough work done before the climate makes it impossible

9 What does he find most attractive about Africa?
a) the way the people live
b) their attitude to older people
c) his work
d) the fact that he can be useful to the community

10 What does he find it most difficult to put up with?
a) the food
b) the heat
c) the lack of opportunities to practice his religion
d) the fact that Africa is changing

11 What does his mother's attitude seem to be?
a) She doesn't appreciate his enthusiasm for Africa.
b) She's afraid to go to Africa.
c) She dislikes the idea of going to Africa.
d) She's glad he's in Africa.

12 What is causing the changes that are taking place in the country, according to the article?
a) the prosperity of Nigeria
b) the discovery of oil in the Sahel

Practice test 5

    c) the end of the drought
    d) modern means of transport

13 What is Willie Russell's attitude to the changes?
    a) They make him unhappy.
    b) He thinks the people will be improved by Westernisation.
    c) He doesn't think it will make any real difference.
    d) He's glad the people will have a better life, even if some things that he loves will disappear.

14 When Willie Russell says 'That's why I came here, isn't it' (at the end of the article), what reason is he referring to?
    a) to see the country before it is too late
    b) to help the country develop
    c) to return to the country of his negro ancestors
    d) to help bring transport and electricity to the country

15 He refers twice to 'the real world'. What do you think he means by this?
    a) a country where people are happy
    b) a country where one's activities and work have some real meaning
    c) a less industrialised world
    d) a country where personal relationships are more genuine than in the United States

---

Practice test 5

Read each text slowly and carefully, and then answer the questions that follow.

First passage

Women's prison goes pop

Prison life will never be quite the same again for women criminals in Scotland.
    The air in their new prison at Cornton Vale, near Sterling, hangs heavy with the perfume of lavender. There are no bars on the windows – just a metal grill.
    Prisoners live on a 'family' basis with their officers, in small units of seven rooms. There is a kitchen where they cook their own meals, and a lounge with fitted carpet and armchairs.
    The 'wakey, wakey' call by loudspeaker at 7 a.m. is followed by a morning music programme featuring the prisoners' favourites.
    Prison authorities and staff dismiss suggestions, however, that Cornton Vale has the atmosphere of a holiday camp. 'This establishment will not be by any means a soft option,' Mr Jack Scrimgeour, director of the Scottish Prison Service, said.
    'Inmates, particularly those with long sentences, will be encouraged to be self-reliant and take responsibility for themselves and others. This is in many ways much more demanding than simply serving time.'

Cornton Vale is the first purpose-built penal establishment wholly for women to be opened in Scotland.

The 220 prisoners at Cornton Vale have single rooms, there is a medical centre, and extensive playing fields. The windows look out over close-cropped lawns and a goldfish pond, with a view of the Ochil Hills. Visiting-day is conducted over a cup of coffee, served by the WRVS.

During the day, most of the prisoners will be employed in three well-lit, cheerfully-decorated workshops, making soft toys or clothing. Their earnings – up to 90p a week – can be spent in the prison shop, in the canteen, or on a 3p hairdo.

The gymnasium, which also acts as a cinema and concert hall, has facilities for table tennis, badminton, keep-fit classes, and dancing.

'We try to preserve human dignity as much as possible, by imagining ourselves in the prisoner's position,' Mrs Agnes Curran, deputy governor, said.
(Report in *The Guardian*)

Choose the answer which you think is most accurate.
1   Cornton Vale is
a) Scotland's first women's prison.
b) Scotland's first prison.
c) Scotland's first prison especially designed for women prisoners.
d) Scotland's first purpose-built prison.

2   Is Cornton Vale easy to escape from, according to the article?
a) The article doesn't make it clear.
b) Yes.
c) No, very difficult.
d) No, impossible.

3   What makes Cornton Vale different from most prisons?
a) the standard of accommodation
b) the attitude of the staff
c) both of these things
d) the fact that prisoners are allowed to work

4   What seems to be the purpose of this prison, according to the article?
a) to help prisoners get through long sentences
b) to make prisoners more demanding
c) to give them a pleasant way of serving time
d) to help them become responsible and independent

5   Who thinks the prison is like a holiday camp?
a) Jack Scrimgeour
b) the prison authorities and staff
c) the prisoners
d) the article doesn't make it clear

6   Who seems to be sent to the prison, according to the article?
a) certain categories of prisoner only
b) prisoners who are given long sentences
c) self-reliant and responsible prisoners
d) all Scottish women prisoners

Practice test 5

7 Units of seven rooms are provided
a) for each prisoner.
b) for groups of prisoners to share.
c) for prisoners and their husbands and children.
d) for specially selected prisoners.

8 What is meant by a 'soft option' (lines 10–11)?
a) an easy way of serving a prison sentence
b) a prison that is easy to escape from
c) a silly idea
d) a friendly gentle place

9 Who is Jack Scrimgeour?
a) the governor of Cornton Vale prison
b) the man in charge of all Scottish prisons
c) the man in charge of Scottish women's prisons
d) one of the staff at Cornton Vale

10 Prisoners who work at Cornton Vale can earn
a) as much as factory workers in ordinary life.
b) just a little money.
c) a normal wage for the work they do.
d) just enough for one hairdo a week.

11 Agnes Curran seems to suggest that if you imagine yourself in the prisoner's position
a) you won't be tempted to commit crimes.
b) you can preserve your dignity.
c) you are more likely to treat prisoners as human beings.
d) you will feel happier.

Second passage

What do prisons do?

At its best, any prison is so unnatural a form of segregation from normal life that – like too-loving parents and too zealous religion and all other well-meant violations of individuality – it helps to prevent the victims from resuming, when they are let out, any natural role in human society. At its worst, the prison is almost scientifically designed to develop by force-ripening every one of the anti-social traits for which we suppose ourselves to put people into prison. (I say 'suppose', because actually we put people into prison only because we don't know what else to do with them...) Prison makes the man who is sexually abnormal, sexually a maniac. Prison makes the man who enjoyed beating fellow drunks in a bar-room come out wanting to kill a policeman...

Probably we cannot tomorrow turn all the so-called criminals loose and close the jails – though, of course that is just what we are doing by letting them go at the end of their sentences. No, Society cannot free the victims Society has unfitted for freedom. Doubtless, since the Millennium is still centuries ahead, it is advisable to make prisons as sanitary and well-lighted as possible, that the convicts may live out their living death more comfortably.

Only keep your philosophy straight. Do not imagine that, when you have by carelessness in not inoculating them, let your victims get smallpox, you are going to save them or exonerate yourselves by bathing their brows, however grateful the bathing may be.

What is to take the place of prisons?

(From *Ann Vickers* by Sinclair Lewis)

12 The author says that prison is like some parents, or like some kinds of religion, in that it
a) makes people incapable of living independently.
b) is too strict.
c) is too kind.
d) doesn't train people for useful work.

13 At the worst, according to the passage, prison
a) makes all prisoners violent.
b) makes criminal characteristics worse.
c) causes sexual problems in most prisoners.
d) destroys the spirit.

14 Why, according to the author, do we put people in prison?
a) to reform them
b) to punish them
c) for lack of any other solution
d) to give them a sense of discipline

15 Why, according to the author, can't we let all the prisoners free?
a) Because we have made them antisocial.
b) Because they are too dangerous.
c) Because they prefer to stay where they are.
d) Because society will not allow it.

16 Read the last sentence but one (beginning 'Do not imagine...'), and then choose the answer which is closest to it in meaning.
a) It is easy to catch diseases such as smallpox in prison.
b) You can't reform prisoners by kind treatment.
c) Society makes criminals; it shouldn't feel it's done enough for them by creating good prison conditions.
d) In any kind of political or social conditions, it is natural that some people should turn out to be enemies of Society.

17 Choose the answer which seems to you to give the best summary of the passage.
a) Some people are natural criminals. It is true that prison makes them worse, but Society cannot be blamed for this – there is no other solution in an imperfect world.
b) Society turns people into criminals, and by putting them into prison it makes them worse. We should make prison conditions as good as possible, but this is by no means our only duty to criminals.
c) Good prison conditions are a mistake: they make it impossible for criminals to adjust to the outside world when they are released. Prison should be severe enough to act like a smallpox inoculation, and so prevent the criminal from catching the 'disease' again.

d) Most crimes involve sex or violence. Prison encourages these, so that criminals are worse when they come out. The only real solution is to keep sexual and violent criminals in prison, in as good conditions as possible, to live out their 'living death'.

Practice test 6

Read the text slowly and carefully, and then answer the questions that follow.

The politics of housework

It seemed perfectly reasonable. We both had careers, both had to work a couple of days a week to earn enough to live on, so why shouldn't we share the housework? So I suggested it to my mate and he agreed – most men are too hip to turn you down flat. You're right, he said. It's only fair.

Then an interesting thing happened. I can only explain it by stating that we women have been brainwashed more than even we can imagine. Probably too many years of seeing television women in ecstasy over shiny waxed floors or breaking down over their dirty shirt collars. Men have no such conditioning. They recognize the essential fact of housework right from the very beginning. Which is that it stinks.

Here's my list of dirty chores: buying groceries, carting them home and putting them away; cooking meals and washing dishes and pots; doing the laundry, digging out the place when things get out of control; washing floors. The list could go on but the sheer necessities are bad enough. All of us have to do these things, or get some one else to do them for us. The longer my husband contemplated these chores, the more repulsed he became, and so proceeded the change from the normally sweet considerate Dr Jekyll into the crafty Mr Hyde who would stop at nothing to avoid the horrors of – housework. As he felt himself backed into a corner laden with dirty dishes, brooms, mops and reeking garbage, his front teeth grew longer and pointier, his fingernails haggled and his eyes grew wild. Housework trivial? Not on your life! Just try to share the burden.

So ensued a dialogue that's been going on for several years. Here are some of the high points:

'*I don't mind sharing the housework, but I don't do it very well. We should each do the things we're best at.*'

MEANING unfortunately I'm no good at things like washing dishes or cooking. What I do best is a little light carpentry, changing light bulbs, moving furniture (how often do you move furniture?).

ALSO MEANING Historically the lower classes (Black men and us) have had hundreds of years experience doing menial jobs. It would be a waste of manpower to train someone else to do them now.

ALSO MEANING I don't like the dull stupid boring jobs, so you should do them.

'*I don't mind sharing the work, but you'll have to show me how to do it.*'

MEANING I ask a lot of questions and you'll have to show me everything everytime I do it because I don't remember so good. Also don't try to sit down and read while I'M doing my jobs because I'm going to annoy hell out of you until it's easier to do them yourself.

'*We used to be so happy!*' (Said whenever it was his turn to do something).

MEANING I used to be so happy.

MEANING Life without housework is bliss. No quarrel here. Perfect agreement.

'*We have different standards, and why should I have to work to your standards. That's unfair.*'

MEANING If I begin to get bugged by the dirt and crap I will say 'This place sure is a sty' or 'How can anyone live like this?' and wait for your reaction. I know that all women have a sore called 'Guilt over a messy house' or 'Household work is ultimately my responsibility.' I know that men have caused that sore – if anyone visits and the place is a sty, they're not going to leave and say, 'He sure is a lousy housekeeper.' You'll take the rap in any case. I can outwait you.

ALSO MEANING I can provoke innumerable scenes over the housework issue. Eventually doing all the housework yourself will be less painful to you than trying to get me to do half. Or I'll suggest we get a maid. She will do my share of the work. You will do yours. It's women's work.

'*I've got nothing against sharing the housework, but you can't make me do it on your schedule.*'

MEANING Passive resistance. I'll do it when I damned well please, if at all. If my job is doing dishes, it's easier to do them once a week. If taking out laundry, once a month. If washing the floors, once a year. If you don't like it, do it yourself oftener, and then I won't do it at all.

'*I hate it more than you. You don't mind it so much.*'

MEANING Housework is garbage work. It's the worst crap I've ever done. It's degrading and humiliating for someone of *my* intelligence to do it. But for someone of *your* intelligence...

'*Housework is too trivial to even talk about.*'

MEANING It's even more trivial to do. Housework is beneath my status. My purpose in life is to deal with matters of significance. Yours is to deal with matters of insignificance. You should do the housework.

'*This problem of housework is not a man–woman problem. In any relationship between two people one is going to have a stronger personality and dominate.*'

MEANING That stronger personality had better be *me*.

'*In animal societies, wolves, for example, the top animal is usually a male even where he is not chosen for brute strength but on the basis of cunning and intelligence. Isn't that interesting?*'

MEANING I have historical, psychological, anthropological and biological justification for keeping you down. How can you ask the top wolf to be equal?

'*Women's Liberation isn't really a political movement.*'

MEANING The Revolution is coming too close to home.

ALSO MEANING I am only interested in how I am oppressed, not how I oppress others. Therefore the war, the draft and the university are political. Women's Liberation is not.

'*Man's accomplishments have always depended on getting help from other people, mostly women. What great man would have accomplished what he did if he had to do his own housework?*'

MEANING Oppression is built into the system and I as the white American male receive the benefits of this system. I don't want to give them up.

(From an article by Pat Mainardi in *Voices from Women's Liberation*)

1   Explain clearly in your own words what you think is meant by the following words and expressions, as they are used in the text.

a) my mate (line 3)
b) hip (line 3)
c) breaking down (line 7)
d) the list could go on (line 12)
e) some of the high points (lines 20–1)

f) menial jobs (line 28)
g) you'll take the rap (lines 43–4)
h) I can outwait you (line 44)
i) I can provoke innumerable scenes (line 45)
j) on your schedule (line 49)
2 Who says the sentences printed in italics?
3 Who is 'us' (line 27)?
4 What does the writer mean by saying that women have been 'brainwashed' (line 6)?
5 What seems to be the real purpose of the person who says 'I don't mind sharing the work, but you'll have to show me how to do it' (line 31)?
6 Who says 'No quarrel here. Perfect agreement' (line 37)?
7 In a paragraph of around 80 words, sum up men's attitude to sharing the housework, according to the writer of the text.

Practice test 7

Read the text slowly and carefully and then answer the questions which follow.

Violence

Four instances of violence come to my mind. One I read about in the newspapers; another I witnessed; in a third I was on the receiving end; in the fourth, the most brutal of them all, I was a perpetrator.

The first took place an hour's drive from my home in Atlanta, Georgia, when a mob in Athens, screaming epithets and hurling rocks, attacked the dormitory occupied by the first Negro girl to enter the University of Georgia.

The second I saw years ago as I walked through a slum area of the Lower East Side of New York: a little old Jew with a beard, pulling his pushcart, was arguing with a Negro who was demanding payment for his work. The bearded man said he didn't have the money and the Negro said he needed it and the argument grew, and the Negro picked up a stick of wood and hit the old man on the side of the head. The old man continued pushing the cart down the street, blood running down his face, and the Negro walked away.

In the third instance, I took my wife and two-year-old daughter to a concert given in an outdoor area near the town of Peekskill, New York. The concert artist was Paul Robeson. As he sang under the open sky to an audience of thousands, a shouting, angry crowd gathered around the field. When the concert was over and we drove off the grounds, the cars moving in a long slow line, we saw the sides of the road filled with cursing, jeering men and women. Then the rocks began to fly. My wife was pregnant at the time. She ducked and pushed our daughter down near the floor of our car. All four side windows and the rear window were smashed by rocks. Sitting in the back seat was a young woman, a stranger, to whom we had given a lift. A flying rock fractured her skull. There were dozens of casualties that day.

The fourth incident occurred in World War II when I was a bombardier with the Eighth Air Force in Europe. The war was almost over. German territory was shrinking, and the Air Force was running out of targets. In France, long since reoccupied by our troops, there was still a tiny pocket of Nazi soldiers in a protected encampment near the city of

Practice test 7

Bordeaux. Someone in the higher echelons decided, though the end of the war was obviously weeks away, that this area should be bombed. Hundreds of Flying Fortresses went. In each bomb bay there were twenty-four one-hundred-pound fire-bombs, containing a new type of jellied gasoline. We set the whole area aflame and obliterated the encampment. Nearby was the ancient town of Royan; that, too, was almost totally destroyed. The Norden bombsight was not that accurate.

    These four instances of violence possess something in common. None of them could have been committed by any animal other than man. The reason for this does not lie alone in man's superior ability to manipulate his environment. It lies in his ability to conceptualize his hatreds. A beast commits violence against specific things for immediate and visible purposes. It needs to eat. It needs a mate. It needs to defend its life. Man has these biological needs plus many more which are culturally created. Man will do violence not only against a specific something which gets in the way of one of his needs; he will do violence against a symbol which stands for, or which he believes stands for, that which prevents him from satisfying his needs. (Guilt by association is high-level thinking.)

    With symbolic violence, the object of attack is deprived of its particularity. Only in this way can man overcome what I believe is his natural spontaneous feeling of oneness with other human beings. He must, by the substitution of symbol for reality, destroy in his consciousness the humanness of that being. To the angry crowds outside the dormitory in Athens, Georgia, their target was not Charlayne Hunter, an extremely attractive and intelligent young woman, sitting, brave and afraid, in her room. She was a 'dirty nigger' – a symbol abstracted from life. To the Negro who committed violence on the streets of New York, this was not a pathetic old Jewish immigrant, forced in the last years of his life to peddle vegetables from a pushcart, but a dehumanized symbol of the historic white exploiter who used the Negro's labor and refused to pay him a just wage. To the screaming rock-throwers of Peekskill who fractured the skull of a young woman returning from a concert, the people in the car they attacked were not a family on an outing; in this car were people who had gone to hear a black-skinned communistic singer and who therefore were all congealed into a symbol representing nigger-loving communism. And as I set my intervalometer and toggled off my bombs over the city of Royan, I was not setting fire to people's homes, crushing and burning individual men, women and newborn babies. We were at war, we always dropped bombs on the enemy, and down there was the enemy.
(From an article by Howard Zinn in *Violence in America*)

1. In the first incident described by the author, why did the crowd attack the black girl?
2. Where is Athens (line 5)?
3. Why did the Negro attack the Jew, in the second incident?
4. Who does the word 'his', in line 9, refer to?
5. In the third incident, why did the crowd attack people leaving the concert?
6. Does the author suggest that it was partly his responsibility that the young woman had her skull fractured?
7. In the fourth incident, why was the author in Europe?
8. What is meant by 'a pocket of Nazi soldiers' (line 26)?
9. Explain the expression 'in the higher echelons' (line 27).
10. Why did the author drop bombs on the town of Royan?
11. What does the word 'that' mean, in line 32?
12. What is the author's purpose in describing the four incidents involving violence?
13. Explain in your own words what the author means by saying that some needs are 'culturally created' (line 38).

14 Say in your own words what the author means by the expression 'symbolic violence' (line 42).
15 According to the author's theory, who was the Negro in the second incident really attacking?
16 What kind of thing (very roughly) do you think an 'intervalometer' is (line 56)?
17 In a paragraph of around 100 words, summarise the four incidents of violence and the author's theory about how they were possible.

Practice test 8

Read the text slowly and carefully and then answer the questions that follow.

How the West was lost

In his book *Bury my Heart at Wounded Knee*, Dee Brown describes the Indian kinship with nature: the land was their mother – 'and one does not sell one's mother'. Yet European notions of property gradually took hold, first with beads, blankets, guns; then fences, enclosures, deeds of purchase. Whole tribes were exterminated; then the buffalo on which they lived. 5
   'The Indians killed only enough to supply their winter needs,' writes Brown, 'stripping the meat to dry in the sun, storing marrow and fat in skins, treating sinews for bowstrings and thread, making spoons and cups of the horns, weaving their hair into ropes and belts, curing the hides for tepee covers, clothing and moccasins.'
   The monstrous slaughter of the buffalo that began in the 1870s had the double purpose 10
of bringing in hides and depriving the Indian of his livelihood. The European hunter left everything but the skin to rot. Nearly four million buffalo were destroyed in two years so that civilisation might advance.
   Even on the reservations, the Indians were not left alone. Corrupt politicians and army officers funnelled in bad food, shoddy blankets and poisonous whisky. If minerals were 15
found, the tribesmen were moved on again. At rare intervals in the story, a protesting white voice is heard. General Sandborn, who headed a peace commission to the Cheyenne after an army massacre of 105 women and children (and 28 men), told Washington: 'For a mighty nation to carry on a war with a few struggling nomads is a spectacle most humiliating, a national crime so revolting that it must bring down on our posterity the 20
judgment of heaven.' Yet Sandborn went on to help the army wipe out the remaining Cheyenne. It took a final piece of planned butchery, in 1890 at Wounded Knee, to end resistance.
   Today, the new militancy is bringing fresh hope and pride to America's 650,000 Indians. But the upsurge of 'red nationalism' is taking many other forms besides simple resistance. In the one-year occupation of Alcatraz the population rose to 800. The spirit of the rock 26
spread over the country: army centres, missile bases, islands and reserves in the U.S. and Canada were occupied; claims were laid to oil-rich lands in Alaska.
   More and more Indians are moving to the cities – there are 60,000 in Los Angeles alone – yet somehow, retaining their Indian identity and pride in their heritage. Others, staying on the reservations, have successfully created their own businesses and industries. The Indian people are also gaining more friends in high places. A champion of long standing

who has acted on behalf of the Sioux and other tribes in the settlement of land claims is presidential candidate Senator George McGovern. 'We must never', he observes, 'repeat in these settlements the exploitation, abuse, and attempted cultural genocide which blots our national heritage.' McGovern has introduced a bill to create an American Indian development bank which would make loans to tribes and the new corporations. He recognises that the Indians resent the paternalism of the Bureau of Indian Affairs, sometimes known as America's colonial service, and feel themselves perfectly competent to run their own affairs.

Almost every day, television perpetuates the myth of the Indian as a savage, to be slaughtered without mercy. In fact, few stereotypes are as false as that of the bloodthirsty Redskin. The Indian is essentially non-violent and civilised, with a deep reverence for nature which makes him a hero and a pioneer in the environmental cause. In a world seemingly hell-bent on self-destruction, the white American is beginning to listen to the placid voice of the Indians.

(Abridged; from an article in *The Observer* Magazine)

1 Say in your own words what was the difference between Indian attitudes to land and those of the white settlers, according to the first paragraph.
2 Explain in your own words why the white Americans destroyed the buffalo.
3 What do you think is meant (roughly) by the expression 'funnelled in' (line 15)?
4 'If minerals were found' (lines 15–16). Found where?
5 Why is it difficult to regard General Sandborn's words (lines 18–21) as completely sincere?
6 When did the Indians stop fighting?
7 What do you think is meant by the expression 'the new militancy' (line 24)?
8 Explain the expression 'retaining their Indian identity' (line 30).
9 What is meant by the expression 'of long standing' (line 32)?
10 What are 'these settlements' (line 35)?
11 What are 'the new corporations' (line 37)?
12 What do Indians dislike about the Bureau of Indian Affairs, according to the passage?
13 What is wrong with the way television presents the American Indians, according to the passage?
14 What is 'the environmental cause' (line 44)?
15 What do you think is meant by the expression 'hell-bent on self-destruction' (line 45)?
16 In a paragraph of about 100 words, summarise what the text says about the history of the American Indians and the efforts that are being made to improve their situation.

Practice test 9

Read the text slowly and carefully and then answer the questions that follow.

Goodbye to the cane*

'If the head says there will be corporal† punishment in the school then you are bound to get unofficial face slapping and hitting with bits of wood, metal, slippers and anything else, all the way down. And if that school shows you its punishment book with one entry a term, then I don't believe it. I know because I went through that.'

Mr David Lewis, headmaster of Redefield secondary school, which serves the huge Blackbird Leys housing estate in Oxford, did not find it easy to get rid of the cane, but he has succeeded and now stands a firmly committed abolitionist.

It was a gradual process with no help from the l.e.a. (Oxford City has only recently decided to abolish corporal punishment in primary and secondary schools as from January). The cane disappeared from the upper school in 1965, much earlier than in the lower school which finally got rid of corporal punishment about three years ago.

The last time Mr Lewis wanted to cane a boy he had difficulty finding a cane. Eventually he found a small dilapidated one meant for junior children and administered the punishment. But he does not think it hurt the fourth former very much.

Mr Lewis became head of the school when it opened as a new secondary modern with only 50 children in 1963. Now it has 788, all but a handful from council houses. Most parents work at the nearby British Leyland Cowley car factory.

Because numbers in the beginning were so small and the growth of the school was gradual, problems of discipline and violence were minimal, and he feels he was luckier than other schools in this respect, particularly with the older children.

However, the discipline of the lower school had been given over completely to the lower school head who believed in corporal punishment. Mr Lewis decided not to interfere. The responsibility, he said, had been delegated and it was 'not up to me to tell him how to do his job'. At that time, around 1966–67, there were about three first and second year children being caned each week.

Most of the staff were in sympathy with the headmaster over corporal punishment – namely that violence on children by teachers did not solve any problems or do any good for the children or the school as a whole. When the particular lower school head left Redefield, corporal punishment stopped. There were no riots; the school continued as normal.

Mr Lewis did not mention it to anyone explicitly. In time, he began to say more and more in conversation with staff or pupils, or at school assembly that he did not like the cane, that Redefield did not have a cane and finally that it never wanted to use the cane.

The hardest period for Redefield was getting the last few teachers to 'cross the bridge' as Mr Lewis puts it. There was then the problem of ensuring that no unofficial corporal punishment went on in the classrooms, and cloakrooms, whether it was ear-clipping or hitting a child with a block of wood. Once the main task has been achieved, coping with the unofficial side is probably the most difficult for any school. Teachers' habits die hard.

While there was no hounding of those few teachers who had their own rules at Redefield, Mr Lewis said it was essential that it stopped because by this time he was openly saying to his children, 'We don't want to hit you because we don't believe in violence and we are not a violent school.'

* *cane*: a stick used in schools for punishing children   † *corporal*: physical

Practice test 10

The fact that Redefield is a happy place to visit is not of course due only to the abolition of corporal punishment. But it is an essential part of the overall philosophy of the school – 'Children must be encouraged to grow up. This means they must be encouraged to have their own dignity and self-respect and must be respected as individuals by us' (extract from the aims and objects of the school issued to staff before they join Redefield). (Report by Mark Vaughan in *The Times Educational Supplement*) 45

1   Who carries out the 'unofficial face slapping' referred to in line 2?
2   What does Mr Lewis mean by saying 'I went through that' (line 4)?
3   What is meant (in this text) by an 'abolitionist' (line 7)?
4   In the expression 'It was a gradual process' (line 8), what does 'it' refer to?
5   Why was Mr Lewis luckier with his discipline problems than other headmasters?
6   What is meant by the word 'delegated' (line 23)?
7   Why did Mr Lewis not at first stop corporal punishment in the lower school?
8   'There were no riots' (line 29). Why might the children have rioted?
9   In the expression 'Mr Lewis did not mention it' (line 31), what does 'it' refer to?
10 Explain the expression 'cross the bridge' (line 34).
11 What is meant by 'the unofficial side' (line 38)?
12 What is meant by 'Teachers' habits die hard' (line 38)?
13 What does 'hounding' mean (line 39)?
14 In the expression 'that it stopped' (line 40), what does 'it' refer to?
15 What else do you think has made Redefield a happy place, apart from the abolition of corporal punishment?
16 In a paragraph of around 100 words, summarise the steps Mr Lewis took to abolish corporal punishment, and describe his attitude to education.

Practice test 10

Read the text slowly and carefully, and then answer the questions that follow.

Schoolbooks and the female stereotype

Illustrations and stories in United States primary school textbooks tend to convince young girls that they should be 'passive' and 'dependent' creatures who need aspire only to lives of service to their future husbands and children, a conference of educators was told here yesterday.

Speaking at the first national conference on schools and sex rôle stereotypes, a University of California professor said a study of the 100 most widely used elementary textbooks demonstrated that girls are constantly depicted as dependent on and subservient to boys. 5

Louise White, of the U.S. Office of Education, told the conference that the female stereotype presented to elementary school children was so overwhelming that by the time most girls reached fourth grade they believed they had only four occupations open to them – nurse, secretary, teacher, or mother. 10

The director of the elementary school textbook study, Lenore Weitzman, of the

Practice test 10

University of California, said that texts in spelling, reading, mathematics, science, and
social studies were examined.

Most stories and illustrations tended to centre on boys rather than girls, and those boys
tended to demonstrate qualities of strength, intelligence, love of adventure, independence,
and courage.

Girls, however, were depicted in passive rôles. Usually they were inside a house, and
often they were helping with housework or playing with dolls.

When boys and girls appeared together in a text, she said, the girls were either watching
the boys do something or they were helping the boys.

Adult men appearing in elementary school texts were depicted in various jobs – astronaut,
truck driver, policeman, cowboy, scientist, banker – in addition to the rôle of father.

But the overwhelming picture of women that emerged from the elementary texts was
that of mother and housewife. Even at that, said Professor Weitzman, the picture was one
of a woman performing simple but time-consuming chores. It failed completely to reflect
the complexities facing a modern housewife.

A study was done by an affiliate of the Central New Jersey National Organisation for
women on 134 books published by 14 major publishing companies and involving 2,760
stories for elementary school children.

According to the findings the composite housewife or mother was a 'limited, colourless,
mindless creature... Not only does she wash, cook, clean, nurse, and find mittens: these
chores constitute her only happiness.

'In illustration, she frequently appears in the servant's posture, body slightly bent
forward, hands clasped, eyes riveted on the master of the house or the children.'

In contrast, the typical father found in the study was 'the "good guy" in the family.
He's where the fun is. He builds things with his children and takes them hunting, fishing
and up in planes. He solves the problems.'

The effect of this on young girls, Professor Weitzman said, is to make them think
their rôle is to serve others. They think they should be attractive so that they can please
others and although they generally have better academic records than boys by the time
they reach adolescence, they value academic and scholastic excellence less than boys do
(Report in *The Guardian*)

1. Where is 'here' (line 3)?
2. What is meant by 'demonstrated' (line 7)?
3. Explain what is meant by the 'female stereotype' (line 9–10).
4. Why, according to the text, do American girls grow up thinking that there are only four possible careers open to them?
5. Explain what is meant by saying that stories 'centre on boys' (line 16).
6. What is meant by the expression 'passive roles' (line 19)?
7. Explain in one sentence the difference in the way boys and girls are presented in American schoolbooks, according to the passage.
8. What is the difference in the way men and women are presented (one sentence)?
9. And the difference in the presentation of mothers and fathers (one sentence)?
10. In the expression 'she said' (line 21), who is 'she'?
11. What is meant by the expression 'the complexities facing a modern housewife' (line 28)?
12. According to the figures given in lines 29–31, roughly how many stories are contained in each book, on average?
13. Is there any contradiction in the passage as regards the number of textbooks examined?

Practice test 10

14 What does the word 'findings' (line 32) mean?
15 What is meant by the expression 'the composite housewife or mother' (line 32)?
16 Rewrite more simply the expression 'in the servant's posture' (line 35).
17 What is meant by saying that girls have 'better academic records' (line 42)?
18 In a paragraph of around 100 words, summarise the results of the investigations into schoolbooks described in the text.

Section D:
Special forms of English

Like any other language, English is used in an enormous number of different situations. This does not normally cause any special comprehension problems – a conversation, a newspaper report, a news broadcast and a letter may be very different in style, but the grammatical structures used will be almost the same in each case. So provided you know your grammar (and have a reasonable vocabulary), you can understand most forms of communication without much difficulty.

However, there are a few situations in which 'normal' English is not used. Newspaper headlines, for instance, are constructed in quite a different way from ordinary sentences (mainly in order to save space), and because of this they can be very difficult to understand. Telegrams also have their own grammar, and so do instructions such as cooking recipes. In this section you will find explanations and exercises which should help you to understand these forms of English more easily.

1   Telegrams

The cost of a telegram depends on the number of words, so naturally people try to use as few words as possible. Articles can almost always be left out of sentences without destroying the meaning, and it is often possible to omit pronouns, possessive adjectives, prepositions, auxiliary verbs and conjunctions. Look at these examples, and try to rewrite them in ordinary English:

>   SEND BLUE SWEATER AND CHEQUE £10
>   UNABLE TRAVEL SATURDAY LETTER FOLLOWS
>   THANKS SUPER WEEKEND WRITING

People usually use the present participle (e.g. 'coming', 'sending') in telegrams to refer to their plans for the future:

>   ARRIVING 2.30 CAN YOU MEET
>   SENDING MONEY TOMORROW ACKNOWLEDGE RECEIPT
>   COMING SATURDAY

(Note that 'COMING SATURDAY' and 'COME SATURDAY' are not the same: 'COME SATURDAY' means 'Please come on Saturday'.)

Exercise a

Write these telegrams in ordinary language:
a) PLANS CHANGED PHONE TUESDAY MORNING
b) IMPORTANT WE MEET SOON PLEASE SUGGEST DATE
c) COME SUNDAY SPEND WEEK BRING GRANNY IF POSSIBLE
d) YOUR OFFER UNACCEPTABLE CANCEL DEAL
e) LEFT PAPERS YOUR HOUSE PLEASE SEND IF FOUND

Special forms of English

    f) THANKS INVITATION REGRET JULY IMPOSSIBLE HOW ABOUT SEPTEMBER
    g) COMING LIVERPOOL THURSDAY ARRANGE MEETING SMITH AND WATSON
    h) THANKS WONDERFUL ROSES DARLING SEE YOU SOON
    i) NEW PROBLEMS ESSENTIAL YOU RETURN SOONEST
    j) ALBERT BORN THURSDAY MORNING BOTH WELL

Exercise b

Write telegrams for imaginary situations that you might find yourself in. For instance, suppose you have all your luggage and papers stolen while on holiday abroad; or you have to tell somebody about an accident; or you want to congratulate somebody on an examination success.

2 Instructions

If you look carefully at instructions written in English (for example, a cooking recipe, the notice in a public telephone box, the directions which tell you how to use a machine), you will often find that the grammar is not quite the same as that of ordinary English. Articles are often left out, for instance:

    'In case of fire, break glass'

Other words may disappear too: in particular, the word 'it' is often omitted:

    'Chill thoroughly before serving'

Exercise c

Read these two short texts carefully, and note how the sentences are constructed. Then write a set of instructions yourself. (Some suggestions: explain how to play a gramophone record, drive a car, shave, wash, boil an egg; give the recipe for a more complicated dish.)

Elastoplast First Aid Plasters

Directions
1. Cleanse wound and surrounding skin carefully.
2. Dry thoroughly – dressing will not adhere in the presence of moisture, grease, powder etc.
3. Remove protective covering and apply dressing to wound.
4. Firmly, but gently press down adhesive edges.

Advocaat Belvedere

Mix together 6 large egg yolks and 6 oz. castor sugar and heat in a saucepan together with 1 large can of evaporated milk until the mixture thickens. Allow to cool, stirring occasionally to stop skin forming. When cool, pour into a bottle and top with brandy to taste. Will keep in a refrigerator for 2–3 days. Costs about 55 p, serves about 8.
(Recipe from *Woman's Own*)

3 Newspaper headlines

British and American newspaper headlines are often extremely hard to understand. Sometimes, of course, this is simply because one doesn't know enough about what's been

Special forms of English

going on in the country recently. Obviously, you can't understand a headline like 'SMITH DOES IT AGAIN!' if you have no idea who Smith is, or what he did the first time. In many cases, however, the problem is a different one: it is that newspaper headlines are written in a special kind of language, almost like a secret code, with its own vocabulary and grammar.

(i) *Vocabulary.* Headlines often contain relatively unusual words which are chosen either because they are short (for example, 'gems', meaning 'jewels'; 'bid', in the sense of 'attempt'), or because they are vivid and dramatic (like 'blaze', which is often used instead of 'fire'). So even if you have a very wide vocabulary, you probably won't be able to understand headlines like 'PRESS CURB PROBE' (meaning 'an investigation into censorship of the press') without a very good dictionary. (To some extent it depends on the paper: the more serious newspapers use less of this kind of language than the others.)

(ii) *Grammar.* Newspaper headlines also have a special grammar, which is different from that of ordinary sentences. The main features of this grammar are: (a) omission of articles and the verb 'to be'; (b) a special tense system; (c) the very frequent use of nouns as adjectives. The following explanations and exercises will help you to deal with these constructions.

The grammar of newspaper headlines

A   Omission of articles and the verb 'to be'

Here are a few examples. The first three are translated into ordinary language; try to translate the others yourself.

ROYAL DOG ILL
One of the Queen's dogs is ill.

MOON AMERICAN, SAYS US SENATOR
A United States senator says that the moon is American.

OPPOSITION CLAIM GOVERNMENT RESPONSIBLE FOR CRISIS
The opposition claim that the government is responsible for the crisis.

DOG WORSE: ROYAL DOCTOR READY TO OPERATE
?

SHAKESPEARE PLAY DISGUSTING, SAYS EDUCATION COMMITTEE CHAIRMAN
?

BRITISH WOMEN MOST BEAUTIFUL IN WORLD, ACCORDING TO MANCHESTER PROFESSOR
?

B   Tenses

Newspaper headlines use a very simplified tense system.

(i) It is unusual to find complex verb forms such as 'is staying' or 'has reached'; generally the simple present form ('stays', 'reaches') is used, whether the headline is about something that has happened, something that is happening, or something that happens

Special forms of English

repeatedly. Look at the following examples, and try to put them into normal English:
    CHINA LAUNCHES SPACE SATELLITE
    STUDENTS FIGHT FOR COURSE CHANGES
    FAT BABIES CRY LESS, SAYS DOCTOR

(ii) Sometimes the present progressive tense is used (particularly to describe something that is developing), but the auxiliary verb 'to be' is left out. Try to rewrite these examples:
    BRITAIN HEADING FOR NEW CRISIS
    WORLD GETTING COLDER, SAY RESEARCHERS

(iii) To refer to the future, headlines usually use the infinitive:
    QUEEN TO VISIT BAFFINLAND
    BRITAIN TO SPEND MORE ON CANCER RESEARCH

(iv) Finally, passive sentences are constructed with no auxiliary verbs – just the past participle. So instead of saying, for example, 'A man *is being held* by the police', the headline would probably say 'MAN HELD BY POLICE'. Headlines like this are easy to misunderstand, if you are not careful. For instance, 'BLACK TEENAGERS ATTACKED IN RACE RIOT' means that the black teenagers *were attacked*, not that they attacked somebody else. If the black teenagers did the attacking, the headline would use the present tense ('BLACK TEENAGERS ATTACK'). Try to rewrite the following headlines in ordinary English:
    NUDE BATHERS PAINTED ON BEACH
    POLICEMAN KILLED IN PUB FIGHT
    LOST CAT RETURNED TO DUCHESS

C Use of nouns as adjectives

Even in ordinary English, it is very common to put nouns before other nouns, as if they were adjectives. For example, a rise in prices can be called a *price rise*; the leg of a table can be called a *table leg*. In newspaper headlines, this often goes to an extreme. Three, four, or even five nouns may be put together into a sort of block, with all the nouns except the last acting as adjectives. Imagine, for instance, that there is a research station in the Welsh mountains trying to develop a waterproof sheep, and that one of the staff turns out to be a spy working for a foreign power. The headline reporting this might compress the essential information into a block of five nouns:
    SHEEP RESEARCH STATION SPY DRAMA

Generally, the easiest way to understand headlines like this is to start at the end and read them backwards: 'BREAD PRICE RISE SHOCK' refers to (1) the shock caused by (2) a rise in (3) the price of (4) bread.

Try to rewrite the following examples in ordinary language:
    SPACE RESEARCH TALKS PROPOSAL
    CAR INDUSTRY UNEMPLOYMENT THREAT
    LIVERPOOL SUPERMARKET BOMB SCARE

Exercise d

Here are some more headlines. Try to rewrite them in ordinary language.
a) SWITZERLAND INVADES NEW ZEALAND
b) WOMAN HELD IN MURDER SEARCH

Special forms of English

c) GIRL, 16, TO ADVISE GOVERNMENT ON TEENAGE PROBLEMS
d) ZOO ESCAPE DRAMA
e) NIGHTCLUB STAR BREAKS LEG
f) POLLUTION DANGER INCREASING, SAY SCIENTISTS
g) BLIND WIDOW CAPTURES TRAIN ROBBER
h) REBEL TROOPS PUSHED BACK IN NEW BATTLE
i) STRIKE THREAT OVER PAY CLAIM REFUSAL
j) EUROPE 51ST STATE, SAYS US GENERAL
k) PIANO FACTORY PAY CUT RIOT DEATH DRAMA
l) CAMBRIDGE UNIVERSITY CASINO PLAN: NEW MOVE

Exercise e

Write some headlines for imaginary newspaper articles about yourself or your friends (For example: 'DUTCH STUDENT TO HITCHHIKE ROUND WORLD'; 'BEAUTIFUL GIRL, 18, HAS TOAST FOR BREAKFAST'; 'HOUSEWIFE GETS LETTER FROM TAXMAN'.)